the girl wants to

the girl wants to

Edited by Lynn Crosbie

Coach House Press

Coach House Press
50 Prince Arthur Avenue, Suite 107
Toronto, Canada M5R 1B5

FIRST EDITION
Published in Canada 1993
Published in the United States 1994
Printed in Canada

*Acknowledgements of permission to reprint material
will be found at the end of the book.*

Published with the assistance of the Canada Council,
the Department of Communications, the Ontario Arts Council,
the Ontario Ministry of Culture, Tourism and
Recreation and the Management Board Secretariat.

Proceeds from this anthology will in part be donated to
the Toronto Rape Crisis Centre.

Canadian Cataloguing in Publication Data
Main entry under title:

The Girl wants to
ISBN 0-88910-462-X

1. Canadian literature - Women authors.
2. American Literature - Woman authors.
3. Erotic literature, Canadian (English) - Women authors.*
4. Erotic literature, American - Women authors.
5. Women - sexual behaviour - Literary collections.
6. Canadian literature - 20th century.
7. American literature - 20th century.
I. Crosbie, Lynn, 1963-

PS8235.W7G5 1993   C810.8'03538   C93-094710-X   PR9194.5.W6G5 1993

To all

the girls

I've loved

before

CONTENTS

Performers

Foreword

How idiotic to say, "No one else needs to do a
book of erotica"! Everyone ought to. How else do
we begin to apprehend, if it is not shown and told,
the full range of this culture's sex?

Carol A. Queen

W HEN I APPROACHED XAVIERA HOLLANDER TO CONTRIBUTE TO THIS
anthology, I told her that I considered her to be an important sex-pioneer. "That's
true," she remarked, "I did take sex, as well as my clothing, out of the closet."
I told Pamela Des Barres and Erica Jong virtually the same thing, because I consider their
work to be courageous and unprecedented in terms of its enthusiastic and *jouissant* accounts
of sexuality. This project has been a labour of love and idolatry for me since its inception, an
inception that began with an examination of my own work, and with a song.

Sylvia Plath once remarked that she had never used the word "toothbrush" in one of her
poems. Conversely, I have always veered away from using explicitly sexual or even modestly
prurient language in my own poetry. Recently, however, I began writing erotic, psycho/sex-
ual work, which prompted me to examine why and how I had achieved this sudden liberty.

I soon realized that my work was informed by a groundswell in women's literature and
art, that the artists I most admired were and are engaged in radical modes of inscribing their
sexuality. Contemporary female-authored alternative comics, fiction, music, fanzines, photography and poetry are currently engaged in an effort to delineate the multiple facets of
female sexuality and subjectivity, an effort that I feel is exciting and imperative. As I began

to assemble contributors, I was haunted by an obscure disco song by Clarence "Blowfly" Reid, entitled "The Girl Wants To Fuck". In this song, Blowfly informs his male listeners that "the girl wants to fuck ... she just can't wait to give all of her pussy away." The song was, for a time, the book's working title: in the interest of feminist reclamation, I decided that the time had come to demonstrate the fact that women have assumed agency and control with regard to what we "want".

I altered the title when I began receiving complex responses to this statement. The women that contributed work interpreted the title, variously, as a call for erotic, sex-positive, raunchy, playful, empowering, critical and ferocious work, thus calling attention to the narrow agenda of my original title.

My original concept ultimately was not altered in the course of compiling the book. I wanted to bring together a selection of artists from diverse media in order to illustrate an implicit collective of women, all of whom are (successfully) struggling to carve their identities as powerful, speaking subjects in the arena of sexuality. I also wanted to draw attention to both famous and infamous women, to Canadian and American artists, and to the infinite ways in which sexuality and power can be imagined and enacted.

The modes, methods, orientations and approaches gathered here are by no means definitive. What this book suggests is that our sexual project is just beginning: its liberating potential is infinite and incalculable. Our movement—from sexual object to subject—is already well under way: I'd like to thank all of the contributors (and many other women) for their tireless, gorgeous and spirited efforts in the name of (to cite Cassie Jameson) G-POWER!

LYNN CROSBIE

ACKNOWLEDGEMENTS

I'd like to thank Alice Palumbo, who assisted me on many occasions

with the production of this book and who provided invaluable suggestions, as well as editorial

and practical assistance. I would also like to thank the following people for their input,

ideas and assistance: Patricia Seaman, Tony Burgess, Steve Goof (Johnston), Dionne Brand,

Ann Diamond, Pamela Lenkov, Jaymz Bee, Andrew Paterson, Daniel Jones,

David Trinidad, Thom Jurek, Ira Silverberg, Steve Banks, Malcolm Ingram, David Demchuk,

Nancy Johnston, Leslie Earl, William New, Jill Ruby, Ellen Flanders, Clint Burnham,

David and Michael McGimpsey, Andrew Brouse, Gail August and James Crosbie.

Finally, special thanks to Laura, Sarah and Margaret.

the girl wants to

Kathy Acker

New York City in 1979

The Whores in Jail at Night

Well, my man's gonna get me out of here as soon as he can.
—When's that gonna be, honey?
—So what? Your man pays so he can put you back on the street as soon as possible.
—Well, what if he wants me back on the street? That's where I belong. I make him good money, don't I? He knows that I'm a good girl.
—Your man ain't anything! Johnny says that if I don't work my ass off for him, he's not going to let me back in the house.
—I have to earn two hundred before I can go back.
—Two hundred? That ain't shit! You can earn two hundred in less than a night. I have to earn four hundred or I might just as well forget sleeping, and there's no running away from Him. My baby is the toughest there is.
—Well, shit girl, if I don't come back with eight hundred I get my ass whupped off.
—That's cause you're junk.
—I ain't no stiff! All of you are junkies. I know what you do!
—What's the matter, honey?
—You've been sitting on the thing for an hour.
—The pains are getting bad. OOgh. I've been bleeding two days now.
—OOgh OOgh OOgh.
—She's gonna bang her head off. She needs a shot.
—Tie a sweater around her head. She's gonna break her head open.
—You should see a doctor, honey.
—The doctor told me I'm having an abortion.
—Matron. Goddammit. Get your ass over here matron!

—I haven't been bleeding this bad. Maybe this is the real abortion.

—Matron! This little girl is having an abortion! You do something. Where the hell is that asshole woman? (The matron throws an open piece of Kotex to the girl.) The service here is getting worse and worse!

—You're not in a hotel, honey.

—It used to be better than this. There's not even any goddamn food. This place is definitely going downhill.

—Oh, shut up. I'm trying to sleep. I need my sleep, unlike you girls, cause I'm going back to work tomorrow.

—Now what the hell do you need sleep for? This is a party. You sleep on your job.

—I sure know this is the only time I get any rest. Tomorrow it's back on the street again.

—If we're lucky.

LESBIANS are women who prefer their own ways to male ways.

LESBIANS prefer the convoluting halls of sensuality to direct goal-pursuing mores.

LESBIANS have made a small world deep within and separated from the world. What has usually been called the world is the male world.

Convoluting halls of sensuality lead them to depend on illusions. Lies and silence are realer than truth.

Either you're in love with someone or you're not. The one thing about being in love with someone is you know you're in love: you're either flying or you're about to kill yourself.

I don't know anyone I'm in love with or I don't know if I'm in love. I have all these memories. I remember that as soon as I've gotten fucked, like a dog I no longer care about the man who just fucked me who I was madly in love with.

So why should I spend a hundred dollars to fly to Toronto to get laid by someone I don't know if I love I don't know if I can love I'm an abortion? I mean a hundred dollars and once I get laid I'll be in agony: I won't be doing exactly what I want. I can't live normally i.e. with love so: there is no more life.

The world is grey afterbirth. Fake. All of New York City is fake is going to go all my friends are going crazy all my friends know they're going crazy disaster is the only thing that's happening.

Suddenly these outbursts in the fake, cause they're so open, spawn a new growth. I'm waiting to see this growth.

I want more and more horrible disaster in New York cause I desperately want to see that new thing that is going to happen this year.

JANEY is a woman who has sexually hurt and been sexually hurt so much she's now frigid. She doesn't want to see her husband any more. There's nothing between them.

Her husband agrees with her that there's nothing more between them.

But there's no such thing as nothingness. Not here. Only death whatever that is is nothing. All the ways people are talking to her now mean nothing. She doesn't want to speak words that are meaningless.

Janey doesn't want to see her husband again.

The quality of life in this city stinks. Is almost nothing. Most people now are deaf-mutes only inside they're screaming. BLOOD. A lot of blood inside is going to fall. MORE and MORE because inside is outside.

New York City will become alive again when the people begin to speak to each other again not information but real emotion. A grave is spreading its legs and BEGGING FOR LOVE.

Robert, Janey's husband, is almost a zombie.

He walks talks plays his saxophone pays for groceries almost like every other human. There's no past. The last six years didn't exist. Janey hates him. He made her a hole. He blasted into her. He has no feeling. The light blue eyes he gave you; the gentle hands; the adoration: AREN'T. NO CRIME. NO BLOOD. THE NEW CITY. Like in Fritz Lang's METROPOLIS.

This year suffering has so blasted all feelings out of her she's become a person. Janey believes it's necessary to blast open her mind constantly and destroy EVERY PARTICLE OF MEMORY THAT SHE LIKES.

A sleeveless black T-shirt binds Janey's breasts. Pleated black fake-leather pants hide her cocklessness. A thin leopard tie winds around her neck. One gold-plated watch, the only remembrance of the dead mother, binds one wrist. A thin black leather band binds the other. The head is almost shaved. Two round prescription mirrors mask the eyes.

Johnny is a man who doesn't want to be living so he doesn't appear to be a man. All his life everyone wanted him to be something. His Jewish mother wanted him to be famous so he wouldn't live the life she was living. The two main girlfriends he has had wanted him to support them in the manner to which they certainly weren't accustomed even though he couldn't put his flabby hands on a penny. His father wanted him to shut up.

All Johnny wants to do is make music. He wants to keep everyone and everything who takes him away from his music off him. Since he can't afford human contact, he can't afford desire. Therefore he hangs around with rich zombies who never have anything to do with feelings. This is a typical New York artist attitude.

New York City is a pit-hole: since the United States government, having decided that New York City is no longer part of the United States of America, is dumping all the laws the rich people want such as anti-rent-control laws and all the people they don't want (artists, poor minorities, and the media in general) on the city and refusing the city Federal funds, the American bourgeoisie has left. Only the poor: artists, Puerto Ricans who can't afford to move ... and rich Europeans who are fleeing the terrorists and who don't give a shit about New York ... inhabit this city.

Meanwhile the temperature is getting hotter and hotter so no one can think clearly. No one perceives. No one cares. Insanity comes out like life is a terrific party.

In Front of the Mud Club, 77 White Street

Two rich couples drop out of a limousine. The women are wearing outfits the poor people who were in ten years ago wore ten years ago. The men are just neutral. All the poor people who're making this club fashionable so the rich want to hang out here, even though the poor still never make a buck off the rich pleasure, are sitting on cars, watching the rich people walk up to the club.

Some creeps around the club's entrance. An open-shirted skinny guy who says he's just an artist is choosing who he'll let into the club. Since it's 3:30 a.m. there aren't many creeps. The artist won't let the rich hippies into the club.

> —Look at that car.
> —Jesus. It's those rich hippies' car.
> —Let's take it.
> —That's the chauffeur over there.
> —Let's kidnap him.
> —Let's knock him over the head with a bottle.
> —I don't want no terrorism. I wanna go for a ride.
> —That's right. We've got nothing to do with terrorism. We'll just explain we want to borrow the car for an hour.
> —Maybe he'll lend us the car if we explain we're terrorists-in-training. We want to use that car to try out terrorist tricks.

After 45 minutes the rich people climb back into their limousine and their chauffeur drives them away.

A girl who has gobs of brown hair like the foam on a cappuccino in Little Italy, black patent leather S&M heels, two unfashionable tits stuffed into a pale green corset, and extremely fashionable black fake leather tights heaves her large self off a car top. She's holding an empty bottle.

Diego senses there's going to be trouble. He gets off his car top. Is walking slowly towards the girl.

The bottle keeps waving. Finally the girl finds some courage heaves the bottle at the skinny entrance artist.

The girl and the artist battle it out up the street. Some of the people who are sitting on cars separate them. We see the girl throw herself back on a car top. Her tits are bouncing so hard she must want our attention and she's getting insecure, maybe violent, cause she isn't getting enough. Better give us a better show. She sticks a middle finger into the air as far as she can. She writhes around on the top of the car. Her movements are so spasmodic she must be nuts.

A yellow taxi cab is slowly making its way to the club. On one side of this taxi cab's the club entrance. The other side is the girl writ(h)ing away on the black car. Three girls who are pretending to be transvestites are lifting themselves out of the cab elegantly around the big girl's body. The first body is encased in a translucent white girdle. A series of diagonal panels leads directly to her cunt. The other two dresses are tight and white. They are wriggling their way toward the club. The big girl, whom the taxi driver refused to let in his cab, wriggling because she's been rejected but not wriggling as much, is bumping into them. They're tottering away from her because she has syphilis.

Now the big girl is unsuccessfully trying to climb through a private white car's window now she's running hips hooking even faster into an alleyway taxi whose driver is locking his doors and windows against her. She's offering him a blow job. Now an ugly boy with a huge safety pin stuck through his upper lip, walking up and down the street, is shooting at us with his watergun.

The dyke sitting next to me is saying earlier in the evening she pulled at this safety pin.

It's four o'clock a.m. It's still too hot. Wet heat's squeezing this city. The air's mist. The liquid that's seeping out of human flesh pores is going to harden into a smooth shiny shell so we're going to become reptiles.

No one wants to move any more. No one wants to be in a body. Physical possessions can go to hell even in this night.

Johnny like all other New York inhabitants doesn't want anything to do with sex. He hates sex because the air's hot, because feelings are dull, and because humans are repulsive.

Like all the other New Yorkers he's telling females he's strictly gay and males all faggots ought to burn in hell and they are. He's doing this because when he was sixteen years old his parents who wanted him to die stuck him in the Merchant Marine and all the guys there cause this is what they do raped his ass off with many doses of coke.

Baudelaire doesn't go directly toward self-satisfaction cause of the following mechanism: X wants Y and, for whatever reasons, thinks it shouldn't want Y. X thinks it is BAD because it wants Y. What X wants is Y and to be GOOD.

Baudelaire does the following to solve this dilemma: he understands that some agency (his parents, society, his mistress, etc.) is saying that wanting Y is BAD. This agency is authority is right. The authority will punish him because he's BAD. The authority will punish him as much as possible, punish me punish me, more than is necessary till it has to be obvious to everyone that the punishment is unjust. Punishers are unjust. All authority right now stinks to high hell. Therefore there is no GOOD and BAD, X cannot be BAD.

It's necessary to go to as many extremes as possible.

As soon as Johnny sees Janey he wants to have sex with her. Johnny takes out his cock and rubs it. He walks over to Janey, puts his arms around her shoulders so he's pinning her against a concrete wall.

Johnny says, "You're always talking about sex. Are you going to spread your legs for me like you spread your legs all the time for any guy you don't know?"

Janey replies, "I'm not fucking any more cause sex is a prison. It's become a support of this post-capitalist system like art. Businessmen who want to make money have to turn out a product that people'll buy and want to keep buying. Since American consumers now own every object there is plus they don't have any money anyway cause they're being squeezed between inflation and depression, just like fucking, these businessmen have to discover products that obvious necessity sells.

"Sex is such a product. Just get rid of the puritanism sweetheart your parents spoon-fed you in between materialism which the sexual revolution did. Thanks to free love and hippies. Sex is a terrific hook. Sexual desire is a naturally fluctuating phenomenon. The sex product presents a naturally expanding market. Now capitalists are doing everything they can to bring world sexual desire to an unbearable edge.

"I don't want to be hurt again. Getting hurt or rejected is more dangerous than I know because now every time I get sexually rejected I get dangerously physically sick. I don't want to hurt again. Every time I hurt I feel so disgusted with myself—that by following some stupid body desire I didn't HAVE to follow, I killed the tender nerves of someone else. I retreat into myself. I again become frigid.

"I never have fun."

Johnny says, "You want to be as desperate as possible but you don't have to be desperate. You're going to be a success. Everybody knows you're going to be a success. Wouldn't you like to give up this artistic life which you know isn't rewarding cause artists now have to turn their work/selves into marketable objects/fluctuating images/fashion have to competitively knife each other in the back because we're not people, can't treat each other like people, no feelings, loneliness comes from the world of rationality, robots, every thing singular, objects defined separate from each other? The whole impetus for art in the first place is gone bye-bye. You know you want to get away from this media world."

Janey replies, "I don't know what I want now. I know the New York City world is more complex and desirable even though everything you're saying's true. I don't know what my heart is cause I'm corrupted."

"Become pure again. Love. You have to will. You can do what you will. Then love'll enter your heart."

"I'm not capable of loving anyone. I'm a freak. Love's an obsession that only weird people have. I'm going to be a robot for the rest of my life. This is confusing to be a human being, but robotism is what's present."

"It's unnatural to be sexless. You eat alone and that's freaky."

"I am lonely out of my mind. I am miserable out of my mind. Open open, what, are you touching me? Touching me. Now I'm going into the state where desire comes out like a

monster. Sex I love you. I'll do anything to touch you. I've got to fuck. Don't you understand don't you have needs as much as I have needs DON'T YOU HAVE TO GET LAID?"

—Janey, close that door. What's the matter with you? Why aren't you doing what I
tell you?
—I'll do whatever you tell me, nana.
—That's right. Now go into that drawer and get that checkbook for me. The Chase
Manhattan one, not the other one. Give me both of them. I'll show you which one.
—I can find it, nana. No, it's not this one.
—Give me both of them. I'll do it.
—Here you are, nana. This is the one you want, isn't it?
—Now sit yourself down and write yourself out a check for $10,000. It doesn't matter
which check you write it on.
—Ten thousand dollars! Are you sure about this, nana?
—Do what I tell you. Write yourself out a check for ten thousand dollars.
—Uh, O.K. What's the date?
—It doesn't matter. Put any date you want. Now hand me my glasses. They're over there.
—I'm just going to clean them. They're dirty.
—You can clean them for me later. Give them to me.
—Are … you sure you want to do this?
—Now I'm going to tell you something, Janey. Invest this. Buy yourself 100 shares of
AT&T. You can fritter it away if you want. Good riddance to you. If your mother had
invested the 800 shares of IBM I gave her, she would have had a steady income and
wouldn't have had to commit suicide. Well, she needed the money. If you invest in AT&T,
you'll always have an income.
—I don't know what to say. I've never seen so much money before. I've never SEEN so
much money before.
—You do what I tell you to do. Buy AT&T.
—I'll put the money in a bank, nana, and as soon as it clears I'll buy AT&T.

At ten o'clock the next morning nana is still asleep. A rich salesman who was spending
his winter in New York had installed her in a huge apartment on Park Avenue for six months.
The apartment's rooms are tremendous, too big for her tiny body, and are still partly unfur-
nished. Thick sick daybed spreads ivory-handled white feather fans hanging above contrast
the black-and-red "naturalistic" clown portraits in the "study" that give an air of culture
rather than of call girl. A call girl or mistress, as soon as her first man is gone, is no longer
innocent. No one to help her, constantly harassed by rent and food bills, in need of elegant
clothing and cosmetics to keep surviving, she has to use her sex to get money.

Nana's sleeping on her stomach, her bare arms hugging instead of a man a pillow into
which she's buried a face soft with sleep. The bedroom and the small adjoining dressing
room are the only two properly furnished rooms. A ray of light filtered through the grey

richly laced curtain focuses on a rosewood bedstead of carved Chinese figures. The bedstead covered by white linen sheets; covered by a pale blue silk quilt; covered by a pale white silk quilt. Chinese pictures, composed of five to seven layers of carved ivory, almost sculptures rather than pictures, surround these gleaming layers.

Nana feels around and, finding no one, calls her maid.

"Paul left ten minutes ago," the girl says as she walks into the room. "He didn't want to wake you. I asked him if he wanted coffee but he said he was in a rush. He'll see you his usual time tomorrow."

"Tomorrow tomorrow." The prostitute can never get anything straight. "Can he come tomorrow?"

"Wednesday's Paul's day. Today you see the furrier."

"I remember," she says, sitting up, "The old furrier told me he's coming Wednesday and I can't go against him. Paul'll have to come another day."

"You didn't tell me. If you don't tell me what's going on, I'm going to get things confused and your Johns'll be running into each other!"

Nana stretches her fatty arms over her head and yawns. Two bunches of short brown hairs are sticking out of her armpits. "I'll call Paul and tell him to come back tonight. No. I won't sleep with anyone tonight. Can I afford it? I'll tell Paul to come on Tuesdays after this and I'll have tonight to myself!" Her nightgown slips down her nipples surrounded by one long brown hair and the rest of her hair, loose and tousled, flows over her still-wet sheets.

Bet—I think feminism is the only thing that matters.

Janey (yawning)—I'm so tired all I can do is sleep all day (only she doesn't fall asleep cause she's suddenly attracted to Michael who's like every other guy she's attracted to married to a friend of hers.)

Bet—First of all feminism is only possible in a socialist state.

Janey—But Russia stinks as much as the United States these days. What has this got to do with your film?

Bet—Cause feminism depends on four factors: first of all, women have to have economic independence. If they don't have that they don't have anything. Second, free daycare centres. Abortions. (Counting on her fingers) Fourth, decent housing.

Janey—I mean those are just material considerations. You're accepting the materialism this society teaches. I mean look I've had lots of abortions I can fuck anyone I want—well, I could—I'm still in prison. I'm not talking about myself.

Bet—Are you against abortions?

Janey—How could I be against abortions? I've had fucking five of them. I can't be against abortions. I just think all that stuff is back in the 1920s. It doesn't apply to this world. This world is different from all that socialism: those multi-national corporations control everything.

Louie—You just don't know how things are cause the feminist movement here is nothing compared to the feminist movements in Italy, England and Australia. That's where women really stick together.

Janey—That's not true! Feminism here, sure it's not the old feminism the groups Gloria Steinem and Ti-Grace, but they were so straight. It's much better now: it's just underground it's not so public.

Louie—The only women in Abercrombie and Fitch's films are those traditionally male defined types. The women are always whores or bitches. They have no power.

Janey—Women are whores now. I think women every time they fuck no matter who they fuck should get paid. When they fuck their boyfriends their husbands. That's the way things are only the women don't get paid.

Louie—Look at Carter's films. There are no women's roles. The only two women in the film who aren't bit players are France who's a bitch and England who's a whore.

Janey—But that's how things were in Rome of that time.

Bet—But, Jane, we're saying things have to be different. Our friends can't keep upholding the sexist state of women in their work.

Janey—You know about Abercrombie and Fitch. I don't even bother saying anything to them. But Carter's film; you've got to look at why an artist does what he does. Otherwise you're not being fair. In ROME Carter's saying the decadent Roman society was like this one.

Louie—The one that a certain small group of artists in New York lives in.

Janey—Yeah.

Louie—He's saying the men we know treat women only as whores and bitches.

Janey—So what are you complaining about?

Bet—Before you were saying you have no one to talk to about your work. That's what I'm saying. We've got to tell Abercrombie and Fitch what they're doing. We've got to start portraying women as strong showing women as the power of this society.

Janey—But we're not.

Bet—But how else are we going to be? In Italy there was this women's art festival. A friend of ours who does performance dressed as a woman and did a performance. Then he revealed he was a man. The women in the festival beat him up and called the police.

Michael—The police?

Janey—Was he good?

Bet—He was the best performer there.

Louie—I think calling the police is weird. They should have just beaten him up.

Janey—I don't like the police.

I WANT ALL THE ABOVE TO BE THE SUN.

Intense Sexual Desire Is the Greatest Thing in the World

Janey dreams of cocks. Janey sees cocks instead of objects.
Janey has to fuck.

This is the way sex drives Janey crazy: before Janey fucks, she keeps her want in cells. As soon as Janey's fucking she wants to be adored as much as possible at the same time as its other extreme, ignored as much as possible. More than this: Janey can no longer perceive herself wanting. Janey is Want.

It's worse than this: if Janey gets sexually rejected her body becomes sick. If she doesn't get who she wants she naturally revolts.

This is the nature of reality. No rationality possible. Only this is true. The world in which there is no feeling, the robot world, doesn't exist. The world is a very dangerous place to live in.

Old women just cause they're old and no man'll fuck them don't stop wanting sex.

The old actress isn't good any more. But she keeps on acting even though she knows all the audiences mock her hideousness and lack of context cause she adores acting. Her legs are grotesque: FLABBY. Above, hidden within the folds of skin, there's an ugly cunt. Two long flaps of white skin spreckled by black hairs like a pig's cock flesh hanging down to the knees. There's no feeling in them. Between these two flaps of skin the meat is red folds and drips a white slime that poisons whatever it touches. Just one drop burns a hole into anything. An odour of garbage infested by maggots floats out of this cunt. One wants to vomit. The meat is so red it looks like someone hacked a body to bits with a cleaver or like the bright red lines under the purple lines on the translucent skin of a woman's body found dead three days ago. This red leads to a hole, a hole of redness, round and round, black nausea. The old actress is black nausea because she reminds us of death. Yet she keeps plying her trade and that makes her trade weird. Glory be to those humans who care absolutely NOTHING for the opinions of other humans: they are the true owners of illusions, transformations and themselves.

Old people are supposed to be smarter than young people.

Old people in this country the United States of America are treated like total shit. Since most people spend their lives mentally dwelling on the material, they have no mental freedom, when they grow old and their skin rots and their bodies turn to putrefying sand and they can't do physical exercise and they can't indulge in bodily pleasure and they're all ugly anyway; suddenly they got nothing. Having nothing, you'd think they could at least be shut up in opiated dens so maybe they'd have a chance to develop dreams or at least they could warn their kids to do something else besides being materialistic. But the way this country's set up, there's not even opiated homes to hide this feelinglessness: old people have to go either to children's or most often into rest homes where they're shunted into wheelchairs and made as fast as possible into zombies cause it's easier to handle a zombie, if you have to handle anything, than a human. So an old person is a big hollow space with nothing in it, just ugh, and that's life: nothing else is going to happen, there's just ugh stop.

Her body takes over.

Anything That Destroys Limits

Afterwards Janey and Johnny went to an all-night movie. All during the first movie Janey's sort of leaning against Johnny cause she's unsure if he's attracted to her and she doesn't want to embarrass him (her) in case he ain't. She kinda scrunches against him. One point Johnny is pressing his knee against her knee but she still ain't sure.

Some Like It Hot ends. All the rest of the painters are gonna leave the movie house cause they've seen *The Misfits*. Separately Janey and Johnny say they're going to stay. The painters are walking out. The movie theatre is black.

Janey still doesn't know what Johnny's feelings are.

A third way through the second movie Johnny's hand grabs her knee. Her whole body becomes crazy. She puts her right hand into his hand but he doesn't want the hand.

Johnny's hand, rubbing her tan leg, is inching closer to her cunt. The hand is moving roughly, grabbing handfuls of flesh, the flesh and blood crawling. He's not responding to anything she's doing.

Finally she's tentatively touching his leg. His hand is pouncing on her right hand setting it an inch below his cock. Her body's becoming even crazier and she's more content.

His other hand is inching slower toward her open slimy hole. Cause the theatre is small, not very dark, and the seats aren't too steep, everyone sitting around them is watching exactly what they're doing: her black dress is shoved up around her young thighs. His hand is almost curving around her dark-pantied cunt. Her and his legs are intertwined. Despite fear she's sure to be arrested just like in a porn book because fear she's wanting him to stick his cock up her right now.

His hand is roughly travelling around her cunt, never touching nothing, smaller and smaller circles.

Morning. The movie house lights go on. Johnny looks at Janey like she's a business acquaintance. From now on everything Janey does is for the purpose of getting Johnny's dick into her.

Johnny, "Let's get out of here."

New York City at six in the morning is beautiful. Empty streets except for a few bums. No garbage. A slight shudder of air down the long long streets. Pale grey prevails. Janey's going to kill Johnny if he doesn't give her his cock instantaneously. She's thinking of ways to get him to give her his cock. Her body takes over. Turn on him.

Throws arms around his neck. Back him against car. Shove clothed cunt around clothed cock. Lick ear because that's what there is.

Lick your ear.

Lick your ear.

Well?

I don't know.

What don't you know? You don't know if you want to?

Turn on him. Throw arms around his neck. Back him against car. Shove clothed cunt

Turn on him.

against clothed cock. Lick ear because that's what there is.

Obviously I want to.

I don't care what you do. You can come home with me; you can take a rain check; you cannot take a rain check.

I have to see my lawyer tomorrow. Then I have lunch with Ray.

Turn on him. Throw arms around his neck. Back him against car. Shove clothed cunt against clothed cock. Lick ear because that's what there is.

You're not helping me much.

You're not helping me much.

Through this morning they walk to her apartment. Johnny and Janey don't touch. Johnny and Janey don't talk to each other.

Johnny is saying that Janey's going to invite him up for a few minutes.

Janey is pouring Johnny a glass of Scotch. Janey is sitting in her bedroom on her bed. Johnny is untying the string holding up her black sheath. Johnny's saliva-wetted fingers are pinching her nipple. Johnny is lifting her body over his prostrate body. Johnny's making her cunt rub very roughly through the clothes against his huge cock. Johnny's taking her off him and lifting her dress over her body. Janey's saying, "Your cock is huge." Janey's placing her lips around Johnny's huge cock. Janey's easing her black underpants over her feet.

Johnny's moaning like he's about to come. Janey's lips are letting go his cock. Johnny's lifting Janey's body over his body so the top of his cock is just touching her lips. His hands on her thighs are pulling her down fast and hard. His cock is so huge it is entering her cunt painfully. His body is immediately moving quickly violently shudders. The cock is entering the bottom of Janey's cunt. Janey is coming. Johnny's hands are not holding Janey's thighs firmly enough and Johnny's moving too quickly to keep Janey coming. Johnny is building up to coming.

That's all right yes I that's all right. I'm coming again smooth of you oh oh smooth, goes on and on, am I coming am I not coming.

Janey's rolling off of Johnny. Johnny's pulling the black pants he's still wearing over his thighs because he has to go home. Janey's telling him she has to sleep alone even though she isn't knowing what she's feeling. At the door to Janey's apartment Johnny's telling Janey he's going to call her. Johnny walks out the door and doesn't see Janey again.

Barbara Wilson

Excerpt from

The Dog Collar Murders

IT WAS LUNCH TIME AND I WENT LOOKING FOR HADLEY. OUTSIDE ONE OF THE rooms in the corridor there was a knot of women, half in, half out of the door, and the noise of raised voices inside. I stopped to ask what was going on.

"It's Miko's workshop," someone said. "It started out with Miko talking about the historical repression of sexuality and the danger of the puritanical wing of the feminist movement trying to stop women from exploring what their sexuality really was. Then she showed two short videos—the first one something from your typical peepshow, with two lesbians making love sort of as a preliminary to the man coming in and giving them what they really wanted. Then Miko showed one of her own videos, which was a lot of revolting-looking close-ups of women's genitals and their hairy legs. And she asked what the difference was.

"Some women shouted that there was no difference, that both were products of the pornographic imagination, which essentially objectifies women and separates their sexuality from their personalities. And other women thought there was a difference—that Miko was showing women the way they really were and not all prettied up for the camera. They thought that Miko's video would actually turn off most male viewers. It turned off a lot of women anyway."

"Is that what they're still arguing about?" I asked.

"No, it's taken a new turn. It started when Miko was talking about being an erotic dissident, and this contingent of women took over and said Miko wasn't really, that she still was representing established notions of sex, that it was just the same old vanilla sex as always. That they were the real sexual outlaws, because they were pushing the boundaries back."

"They're the S/Mers," someone else said. "One of them's even wearing a dog collar with a leash attached."

"This I have to see," I said and squeezed into the room.

Nicky Kay, the woman I'd seen at the Espressomat the other day, was standing up in front of the roomful of women and talking. I hardly recognized her. Gone were the Oxford shirt, jeans and glasses. She was wearing a silky sort of see-through dress with black lacey underwear and a garter belt holding up sheer black stockings. Her eyes were heavily made-up, she had a hectic flush to her cheeks and around her neck was a dog collar, black leather studded with silver spikes, the leash dangling over one shoulder. Next to her stood Oak, in black leather pants and a leather vest with no shirt underneath, wearing heavy black boots. On her wrists were wide leather bracelets with studs.

"Most of you know nothing about S/M and yet you condemn it," Nicky was saying. "What is it you're so afraid of? The lesbians here talk about being a minority sexual community and yet they refuse to allow us to have a forum to speak. Christians Against Pornography is invited to speak on a panel—not even about sexuality, but about pornography—but we're not invited. Why are we so threatening? I'll bet most of you haven't even thought about it. You take your cues from the rest of society, which is repressive and puritanical. You take your cues from the wave of the feminist movement that says sex is something that men do to us, that women don't like. Even the lesbians here are ashamed of female desire—or their lack of it. A lot of lesbians became lesbians for political reasons, not because of being attracted to women. It's that wing of the feminist movement that doesn't want us to speak our desires, that wants to silence us!"

"S/M isn't about sexuality, that's why!" Someone shouted back at Nicky. "It's about degradation and patriarchal power and woman-hating!"

I saw Hadley over in a corner of the room and tried to move in her direction.

"S/M is about power, that's true, but it's about the flow of power. Power in heterosexual relations is frozen and static, with one side always dominant and one side always submissive. S/M is about movement and the exchange of energy."

Oak took up her line smoothly. "Unlike in the so-called real world, nothing in S/M is ever done without the consent of both people. That makes things a lot clearer and cleaner. There's a lot less of the emotional bullshit and power games between S/M dykes than between vanilla dykes."

"Sex between most lesbians isn't mutual," affirmed Nicky. "It's just a trade-off, first me, then you. But in S/M the possibility exists of opening all the way up, breaking limits you thought you had, satisfying yourself and your partner with incredible erotic intensity."

In spite of myself I was listening hard. That part sounded great. But ...

"Why don't you talk about the pain and humiliation, Nicky?" A woman asked. "About women with scars from razor blades all over their breasts, about women who've had internal hemorrhaging from being fist-fucked. About women who have to eat shit and drink urine. Don't just talk about power and trust; talk about broken arms and whip marks and burns from hot wax."

"S/M is about safety," Nicky said, two hot stains of red in her cheeks. "And you ought to know—you did it for years!"

Shock and scandal. The speaker was a well-known lesbian therapist.I was still trying to get to Hadley. Over in the corner of the room I could see her familiar silver-blond head and straight nose.

"That's why I know about S/M from the inside," said the therapist bravely. "I know what a lie it is and how it perpetuates the idea that degradation is acceptable and even good. Some women who've been sexually abused get into it as a way of trying to work through old feelings and to conquer them. I know, I was one. But it doesn't work, it's never going to work."

The room was buzzing. It was strange that Miko seemed to have retreated and was letting Nicky just take over like this. Maybe she was filming it from somewhere.

"Oh Christ, let's not be so melodramatic and hypocritical," said Nicky. "I bet three-quarters of you in this room have had rape fantasies, or fantasies of being tied up or forcing someone against her will. Let's be honest for once, okay, and not put it all on us. We're simply the most outspoken, but I bet most of you here have turned yourself on to some kind of S/M fantasies at one time or another."

Did she want a show of hands? She wasn't going to get it in this charged atmosphere. Instead, people seemed to be giving credence to Nicky's charge of hypocrisy and to be avoiding each other's eyes and trying to sneak out the door.

I moved to the back of the room through the gaps, and finally got close to where Hadley was. And Miko. Now it was obvious why Miko hadn't been participating in the discussion. She was whispering in Hadley's ear, and her hand was on Hadley's thigh.

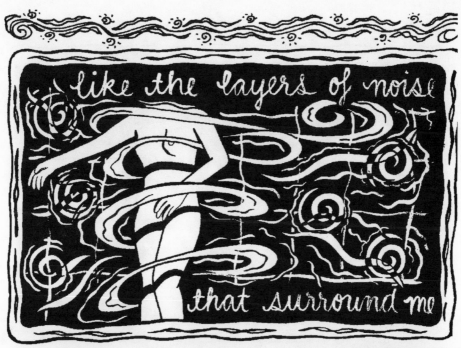

Nicole Brossard

Reverse/Drift

and touches magically
the consenting skin
all the spells that cross it
and circulate slow curves
in the forbidden areas
give your consent
so that the beast becomes enamoured
of strangeness and lifts its claws
to your neck

you reveal yourself without motive muscle
you scrape the curves
and in the rhythm let yourself
bend and dance the charms
she-wolf out of place in the season
adrift on the horizon
a slow image of pleasure

black quiver oh move persuasive
the words desire and me blindly
the passing effects which arouse
reawaken the claws which incline one
to open and celebration between the teeth
the hair and dark set off
out of control

strength of connection of moving lips
cast us adrift reverse the pauses of love
since with time silence
breath shields herself and bites

and slowness nestles down
the hair
awakening ravenous unleashed
our strategy
the seduction swerved

beast looms in the place
cuts off meaning devours
and restores the contours
of the unit
the image in the shadowy light
asleep to the missing sun
....
if come close insist as if to seduce
and to melt together afterwards
useless among the other words
then the shoulder falls asleep and seeks
no other victim to overturn through
pleasure and privation

    Translated by Larry Shouldice

A Rod for a Handsome Price

(from her to ravish meaning ravine. On the other side artifice slumbers in the green. The
shadow follows hour by hour hollow and gloomy and which call me forth)
...........................grafted onto the sentence
o a long time distant to hang on my belly obscure parallel
images and tattoos age suggestive of the fingernail grazing
the thigh the valley get turned on

the body gentle with daring
drug to take away her meaning
her skin of orange and olive
her texture of assailing couple
(you underline them with a stroke
like the bed under their weight
their pleasure)

.............and plunge down
and so body to body in the tuft
her spreading out in vegetation
right to them
the point of consent and
affirmation

little magic boxes.............

the skin a free grammar
of silence canvas of impressions of
representation
fire: artifice a distance
the true skin strips off the vowels
illustrate
the soft sponges or the fine cob

the definite connection that exists
between ravishing meaning from her and
magic boxes

A ROD FOR A HANDSOME PRICE swells
(but)
since the grafts
gently the words run
along it quietly

Translated by Larry Shouldice

CHAPTER II

Alexandre was madly in love with his sister Marielle. He'd never been able to understand why everything went on in him as though he wasn't free to stop loving the woman who, as he said himself, was really pretty ordinary. After all. For him it certainly wasn't just a magical mystery love.

By 1973, Montreal for us was finished with. A city that had nothing left to say to us. There came a point where Lucy thought she'd try exploring it from stem to stern, see what it would stimulate, becoming one with it house by house, a patch of shadow or a patch of wall. She swelled up with analogies before our eyes. At the drop of a hat she'd trip off to the farthest reaches of her soul.

So we were happy all this time, like believers taking first communion. Affectionate celebrants. Orgiasts. Searchers without precise aims. Prospectors for that seam of gold. The one obsession we couldn't escape was the city and its streets, which we roamed on foot, by bus, by taxi, in Violet with all her giddy turns along the way. Pranksome car. Once we rented three motor bikes for two days. We roared athrob all over the place. Potholes, oily patches on the pavement, perilous pebbles in back lanes. Marielle, alone on her bike one day, invited a little tyke of ten to ride behind her and all day long he stayed with us, leading us to discoveries. Spaces. Quarry in two senses. Sand.

We had an impression five years long that someone was telling us a story. One we believed. We filled the gaps and scratched out the repetitions that didn't suit our exploratory wants.

What our bodies did and how they worked fascinated us as well.

None of us was ever sick through those five years. But we felt, or rather we were sure we knew our bodies, exploring every last recess. To the very core. In pleasure and in pain, when for example we didn't realize one's body could feel orgasms suddenly and incidentally. That nipped in the bud our blossoming to realities that were new. Ones already there. But for us still new, enigmatic, erectile ones.

In 1977, Marielle had a child by Alexandre. At first we thought that would end it all. That we'd go back to what we'd been. Back to our offices and factories. All five of us were present for the birth. Two li'l daddies, two li'l mammies, we bawled like frightened kids while Marielle breathed in and out, blowing her best on that ember of life. Her contractions, rhythms, relaxations.

Elle and Lexa weren't a couple. We were a five-some. Utopians living on the fringe, roving full of dash and flash, feeling life and all its secretions moving inside of us. The inner alchemies left us limp with willingness.

Yet there came a time of some anxiety. Reality was slipping from our grasp. Fiction was taking hold of us. Like a spell. What magic potion had we drunk? Or was it Montreal that kept changing and making us think it was one long hallucination we were in?

Excerpt from **French Kiss**, *translated by Patricia Claxton*

Ann Diamond

A Journal of Mona

NOW THAT MONA'S GONE, I FEEL THE NEED TO RECONSTRUCT HER. IT'S NOT that we were great friends. Even if there had been time for that, I doubt if either of us would have been up to it, myself least of all. It's not that I admired her particularly, either. I found many things about her tediously adolescent. I don't mind if people are loaded with contradictions, as long as they stop somewhere short of hypocrisy. But Mona had to lead a double life while I was around: living up, on one hand, to my expectations of her, and keeping pace, on the other, with her own raunchier impulses. Sometimes I felt guilty for coming in the way I did, saying to her, the day after our first meeting at a party, "I want to write about you." She was so enthusiastic. I began to suspect my own motives.

She was thin, with hollow cheeks and deep eyes like pools of accusation. The hems of her dresses were threadbare and her clothes hung on her like loose pyjamas, tattered and clownish. She was not beautiful, with her slightly crooked nose and too-short upper lip. But there was something subtly irresistible about her, a facility she had, I believe, for coming into a person's life and imperceptibly twisting it out of shape.

She had a banner across one whole wall of her downtown studio, on which were printed the words: "I AM THE WHORE OF EXISTENTIAL LONELINESS." I liked that phrase.

Perhaps the most affecting thing about her, as a person and as a dancer, was how she walked the tightrope of her own solitude. She had been married but was recently separated, with a six-year-old daughter. Whether expounding on the need for children's pornography or performing a striptease for an audience of close women friends, she was always topical, always precariously balanced.

At the beginning she told me everything she could think of that would help me to understand her and later describe her: every bit of banal fact. There were times when I could have cried over her innocence. Some of her statements were so well thought out, so carefully phrased they were almost perfect and so transparently false that I felt uncomfortable about being given such intimate access to the character behind the façade.

She did not talk very much about her experiences as a prostitute, and I was shy about asking, for fear of seeming too eager and naïve. Perhaps all along I somehow sensed that she was not really a prostitute. If she were a real prostitute, I doubt that it would have been so easy to talk with her. About politics, for example; or about the dissolution of the boundary between life and art, an area in which she considered herself a sort of connoisseur. She would have been too busy, to begin with.

On the day we had arranged to meet for an interview, I called her up, but she was pretending not to be home.

"Hello," I said. "Mona?"

"*Je ne suis pas Mona,*" she said in a phoney soprano. "*Je suis Monique. Qui parle?*" Her accent was *atroce,* as they say.

"Come on, Mona," I said. "This is Anne." There was a suspicious-sounding pause. "I was hoping we could get together ...."

A sigh of relief. "Oh, it's you. I thought it was the bank." Two days before, one of the tellers had deposited sixty dollars in her account by mistake. She had no idea they would discover the error so soon. She tried to return the merchandise, but it had been on sale. Now the bank was calling her every half hour.

She was playing with eggs in preparation for a performance with eggs which she planned on giving some afternoon in her studio. Just then her daughter cracked one by mistake, thinking it was hard-boiled.

"Don't touch those eggs!" shouted Mona, with her hand over the receiver. "I know how to play with them and you don't!"

This was the first hint of the series of distracting circumstances which always interrupted our interviews. Later I learned to ignore them, because the slightest acknowledgement tended to inflate them into subjects for hour-long conversations, or monologues I should say. And it was hard to interrupt Mona once her indignation had been aroused over some small incident.

But that day I was excited and curious, and when I arrived at the top of her three flights of stairs (she lived on the top floor of a commercial building) I was overjoyed to find her sitting amid stacks of papers and photographs, apparently very ready to talk. I could see she had a great love of publicity. She was ready to turn over everything to me: diaries, poems, personal letters from friends. Her life, she said, was best understood as collage.

Her place had the disordered fluidity of a child's playroom, and the open space that was supposed to be for dancing was always cluttered with clothing, sheets of paper, bits of junk. Her front window overlooked a strip of nightclubs and smoked-meat restaurants; after dark, neon played on the wall over her bed, which was in one corner of the room on the floor.

We talked at random at first. I stammered out my intentions. I was not a professional, I said. She said that was all right: neither was she, she said. The idea of a collaboration interested her. It was to be a sort of temporary marriage: her wild, unexamined career to my cool perspicacity.

I was nervous at first about interviewing her. First there was the problem of getting to

I AM THE WHO

XISTENTIAL LONELINESS

know her, of becoming her friend, so that later on there would be no question of prying into her secrets. Sometimes I felt dishonest, even though I thought my intentions had been well enough explained. In the back of my mind I felt a constant, nagging question: what were my intentions? Quite early on in our discussions I realized things were not going well. There was a strange resistance, a tendency to talk too fast and too loud, as if neither of us really wanted to be understood.

Mona noticed it, too. "We need a third person," she said. "Someone to be a buffer, because you and I are both very aggressive. We're too much alike."

I was doubtful. But as these things happen, one afternoon Mona's old lover, Nessia, turned up while I was walking into Demos' restaurant and led me to her special table in the back, near the toilets.

She talked to me through mouthfuls of Greek salad, brought to her free of charge by the owner, as part of his ongoing payment to her for a portrait she had painted of his wife. "What you must learn first about Mona," she said, "is that she is no prostitute. She is a pseudo-prostitute. She likes to brag to people that she is a prostitute, but when is she a prostitute? Two or three times a year? At the most. And even then, she is a lousy prostitute. I used to pimp for her, and I've seen at first hand how she operates. Pathetic. I would stand behind the curtain while she talked to the man, with one hand over my mouth to keep from screaming!"

I had met Nessia only once, the week before, as I was leaving Mona's place, and then only for two or three minutes. She was about thirty and very tiny, some fiery mixture of Armenian and Egyptian. Here in front of me at the table, she was crouched like a wild animal over her bowl of lettuce. She had a strange, distracting way of smacking her lips every time she had to breathe in mid-sentence. It reminded me of the involuntary growls and cries a cat makes when it sees a bird it can't get at. I found it surprising that so much tense aggression could inhabit one small female body.

"And another thing about Mona," she was saying. "She is arrogant and violent. When she doesn't like what you are saying to her, she will just slap you. Not you, perhaps, because you are taller than she is. But me she likes to slap, because I am small. Once we were talking and suddenly she slapped me, very hard. My head was ringing, but I made sure she would never do that again. I knocked her down. I said, 'If you ever SLAP me again, you will be very sorry you have done it.' After that she was more polite with me."

I nodded and smiled and continued to eat my salad. I had nothing to add to this conversation. Nothing in my experience of Mona quite compared with it.

"Come to my studio some time," said Nessia. "I would like to paint your portrait. Why do you want to write about Mona? I happen to know a very great deal about Mona. And I know more about prostitutes than Mona will ever learn in a lifetime. I have known prostitutes all over the world. In Mexico, I lived with prostitutes. There the police act as pimps. But Alexandria—Alexandria has the most beautiful prostitutes of any city. I have slept with prostitutes in cities on three continents. They are all remarkable women."

Her eyes grew nostalgic, then sharpened again. "In fact," she said, "if you would like to meet a real prostitute, I am going to see one tomorrow night. Would you like to come and

I AM

watch us?" She narrowed her eyes and rumpled her hair with one hand as if something about me had just struck her as hilarious and she needed this gesture to recover her composure. "She is a very interesting woman. She is from France. I met her last week while I was walking down Lagauchetière Street. She leaned out of the window as I was passing by and held her arms out to me.

"'*Oh, mon pauvre petit, tu as l'air vraiment seul!*' That's what she said to me, what do you think of that? Then she said, 'Oh! You're a woman. I thought you were a young boy. But it doesn't matter! Come home with me anyway!'

"Would you like to meet her? I will introduce you to her. You will like her very much. She is an anthropologist."

I thanked her and took down her address dubiously. She lived at the Lido Tourist Rooms.

I was not quite ready to betray Mona's myth about herself by forming a friendship with Nessia. But I was bewildered by this new information. That evening I went for our interview, as we had arranged the week before. Mona was the same as always, but I found it difficult not to feel a kind of guilty pessimism. I had uncovered a shameful double negative. How, I wondered, could a woman pretend to be a prostitute? Wasn't it enough just to be one? Why counterfeit something which was itself so complex a mixture of realism and deception? It seemed middle class to me, this great concern for maximum shock effect which left so many loopholes in case the need arose to escape to a more decent image and lifestyle.

But I couldn't tell Mona that, of course. So a shady kind of deception crept into our friendship. I found myself watching for the contradictions in her stories, suspecting more and more that her fabric of lies was too tightly interwoven with the rest of her. I couldn't interfere with something so visceral. Subtly, I began to disengage myself.

Some time between our third and fourth meeting, Mona moved from her studio. When I next saw her she was staying with three women who had a house on a well-kept boulevard in an old section, half an hour's walk from downtown. As I came through the door she was standing by the piano in a room with hanging plants and a green carpet. She looked nervous and radiant. Her daughter was at school that day; Mona had just sold half her belongings and was preparing to leave any day for California.

"I had a dream," she said, "about my husband. My ex-husband. I thought I should tell you, in case it helps explain something. I dreamed he had drowned and was washed downriver over a stretch of rapids. When I heard about it I felt I should look for him, so I went wading in the calmer water below the falls, searching for traces of his body, but there were none. He had dissolved, without leaving any sign that he had ever lived at all."

"How does that make you feel?" I asked.

"It makes me feel free," she said.

At times Mona still looked to me like a woman who had been given a special glimpse into the deeper mysteries of a continent, a visa into men's unconscious. There was a moment when I thought I had come to understand her as her mythic self, but it came and went too quickly, like her spells of lucidity. Afterwards she never again could seem quite so wise or so eloquent, and my faith in her took a downward turn as her behaviour grew more and more predictably chaotic. I had too easily found the point where her vision seemed to fail, where she became a figure trapped in her own gyrations. But it would have shocked her if I had told her that conscious choice, not oppressive circumstances, was the cause. Maybe my lack of faith, in the end, was what drove her farther into fantasy and narcissism. If she had at first looked to me as someone who would help her explore that world, then I let her down badly. But she soon found someone more tangible and willing in the person of a woman called Rose.

"Let's talk about Rose," I said one day, a week later, when I had my tape recorder. Mona's eyes narrowed with suspicion.

"Why, all of a sudden, do you want to talk about Rose? The last time I saw you, you didn't want to know from Rose."

That was true. My attitude had changed. But the last time we were together, all she wanted to talk about was Rose. How she loved Rose. How Rose drove her crazy. Because Rose was crazy, certifiably cuckoo. That didn't bother me so much, I know plenty of crazy people. But I thought their relationship was unhealthy, lopsided, destructive. And based mostly on the fact that Rose couldn't speak English, while Mona's French was just a notch or two above rudimentary. A physical attraction can last a long time when you don't understand what a person is saying to you.

"Oh, I guess you haven't heard," said Mona. "She was in the hospital. I had to have her committed. But now she's out again, and everything's back to normal."

Some friends of Rose had gone to get her in her friend, Lucie's, car. Lucie and Mona and a woman named Ghiselaine. When they got to the hospital, this rescue party of her lovers and ex-lovers, she was sitting in the recreation area and was very, very calm. They all sat down for a while, trying to talk to her, until finally Lucie said, "Rose, you don't have to stay here if you don't want to." Rose didn't know that. In fact, it came as quite a surprise to Mona, too. Lucie went to get some papers for Rose to sign and came back with a nurse. Rose signed herself out, and the rest of them signed as witnesses, and then the three of them took Rose away.

But on the way back, seated in the front beside Lucie while Rose sprawled and slept on Ghiselaine's lap in the back, Mona had started to feel a bit uneasy about their good deed. She leaned over and whispered to Lucie, "Lucie, don't tell Rose the address of the place where I'm staying this month. I don't think I could handle her coming around."

"You know," said Mona, making a face at me, "I could just see her coming and burning bits of paper in the living room here, when the other people were home. They're not the type that would understand."

Rose was still drowsy from the hospital medication, but as they drove through downtown Montreal, she began to insist that they take her to Jilly's bar. They took her, and of course a crowd of her old friends was there. She sat with some of the women she knew and drank beer until five in the morning, when someone carried her home. A couple of days later she turned up at Mona's new residence, as crazy as ever.

Mona and Rose. An unlikely combination, you'd have thought, if you'd known as little

LONELINESS

about Mona as I did when she and Rose first met. I recall that night very well. It was the night Mona performed a strip act for a women's dance in a church basement. I arrived just before she came on stage, in an all-black costume, a skirt with side slits, widebrimmed hat, long black gloves. First she took off her hat and peeled off the gloves. Ten minutes later she was down to her lace corset. Then the stockings came off, the best part of all: it was obvious that she knew how to take off stockings. Above the sound of the music, a few women whistled and cheered. At the end Mona stood alone on the floodlit stage completely naked: smiling wickedly, I thought. I cheered, but it was hard not to notice a certain sarcasm emanating from Mona.

Afterwards I went to kiss Mona goodbye and bumped into Rose, standing with cap outstretched like a *petit bonhomme*. I had never seen her before, but she was the sort of person you would remember. She had short dark hair, smoky-looking eyes, full lips; she was, you would say, intensely sensual, with everyone. "*As-tu quelque chose pour la danseuse?*" she asked, gesturing at Mona, who had slipped back into her satin costume and was talking to some women from the audience. She leaned close to me, almost breathing the words in my ear. I gave her a dollar and walked toward Mona, who was still talking—tight-lipped and not exactly a picture of artistic triumph. I went out without saying goodbye.

The next time I went to visit Mona, Rose was there, wearing an unbuttoned Chinese silk bathrobe, stepping barefoot among the pieces of her shattered guitar, which lay all over the floor of Mona's studio. She had had a bad night, Mona told me. Rose was talking to herself like a child in the aftermath of an air-raid: she seemed that detached and dazed.

"When I agreed to strip at that women's dance," said Mona, reminiscent, into my tape recorder, "I knew I was about to invoke something beyond the normal. And sure enough, I invoked Rose." There was a note of satisfaction in her voice. I wanted to let the subject drop there, to spare myself some irritation, but Mona refused to let it lie.

"Rose," she insisted, "is very interesting. She talks about nuns all the time. She's reacting against things which hardly exist for most North Americans, or for us."

"Us?" I said. "How can you say '*us*'? You're an American. I was born here. I know all about this stuff, even if I'm not French or Catholic."

"I don't think you could ever understand Rose," said Mona, giving me one of her cool narrow looks.

But then I didn't know Rose. How could I argue with her? I was speechless for a moment, and yes, even a little hurt.

But I wasn't blind to the fact that Mona had become very philosophical about Rose's illness, now that Rose had been gotten more or less out of the way. She talked about how Rose needed therapy and support, from people who would accept her "as a lesbian." She launched into a bitter critique of the medical establishment. "Why isn't there a psychiatrist in this city who will help her without asking her to change what she is?" she demanded to know.

"In other societies," she said, "more humane societies than this one (primitive societies, for instance), people like Rose are not outcasts just because they have to make a total revolution in themselves every ten days or so. They're accepted and given useful work to do."

"Like what kind of work?" I asked.

"Well, like carrying the mail over the mountains or something."

So much for the pontifications of dancers and social rebels. But for all her human failings, I still liked Mona. Then, too, there wasn't so much time that I could afford to waste it haggling over petty differences. Mona was going down to California to visit her parents and might never be back.

Who can tell? The character of Mona might suddenly revert to its original elements, there in the place where she grew up. She might put on weight, become prosaic, melt into the geography of Palo Alto forever. The Mona we knew might be on the brink of extinction; perhaps all along she has only mirrored the seamier side of the city she adopted as her very own, and in which she was a kind of guiding light these past two years. Perhaps with the woman gone, only the myth will remain. That's why my work is so important, though as her biographer, I feel I am failing in my responsibilities. I'm losing my grip on the facts. I am failing to uncover the truth, and the truth, when I do uncover some of it (which is rarely), always disappoints me.

Mona is a woman who has involved herself in Mystery, but most of the time she seems most involved with the utterly disintegrative mysteries. I am afraid that this has a contagious aspect and may be the whole basis of my attraction to her. She has headed for the absolute.

I have read her notebooks, beginning with the year of her daughter's birth, leading into the period when she first began dancing in clubs. Even her handwriting falls apart on the page, once she begins the dancing. She calls it her "liberation from linear thought". But to me it's all too disturbing and evident: I can follow the process, how she seems to vanish as the subject of her own writing. The more she is immersed in the strippers' world, the more her diary becomes a kind of tapestry of different voices: voices from the club, the pimps and the customers; voices of various inner demons. As though, in recording them all almost randomly as she seems to have done, she were indicating her own

A physical attraction can last a long time when you don't understand what a person is saying to you.

readiness to obey any of them.

"A woman," she says, "is a receptacle. There's nothing degrading about that. When she's dancing, she's a receptacle for whatever she chooses."

Her love of chaos keeps me on the defensive.

But she has made me aware that some day prostitution, the myth she expounds, may replace the myth of marriage. Mona is not the only woman for whom all men have begun to resemble pimps. As she says, in effect: Smash the State in the long run. But in the meantime, stay alive by turning tricks. Be a parasite on the people who oppress you: kill them slowly by feeding on them. Prostitution is simply the most obvious recourse for a generation of women schooled in the belief that love is a con.

The last time I had a chance to talk with her for any length of time, she was rehearsing for a performance in Toronto, at another women's dance. Our talking that night relieved her nervousness and took her mind off the show she hadn't yet prepared.

"Is there," she asked, as if she vehemently desired an answer, "a female anti-hero? Or are there just anti-heroes' whores?"

I didn't know. I said I thought it wasn't likely that a woman could ever allow herself to be as nihilistic as one of Céline's male characters. There was the species to think of. She seemed dissatisfied.

Nothing went well that evening. She fell apart before my eyes, standing there in her clown make-up. "I haven't rehearsed," she wailed. She'd spent all her time with lovers, and the show was tomorrow night.

I said, "Just do anything. Those women will be so surprised it won't matter what you do. Do a stocking act."

But she wanted to make a statement about androgyny. The insolubility of it paralyzed and depressed her. I knew she wanted me to get up and dance with her, but I was immobilized by the spectacle she made, and by something else.

She sat down, drooping, eyes on the floor, looking like a delicate girl or a clown in the tragic sense. A woman trying to find the pieces of herself for the life-or-death performance. I found myself talking about solitude. Outside the window the bars of downtown were lighting up for the evening, and voices drifted up from the street.

When desire has gone from a situation, all you can do is obey your instinct for duty, leave nothing unfinished. Be constant, be reasonable. To the best of my ability I was. I found I was waiting for Mona to leave so that I could immortalize her with impunity. I needed time to recover.

The day before her departure, she called me up. We went walking. Mona said, "I had a dream about you."

"Oh?" I said.

"You were talking with that man you told me about, the one you're being 'faithful' to. He was asking you about me. All I remember you saying was: '*Oh, I think it's terribly unnatural.*'"

She looked at me with an odd smile on her lips. I just smiled and shook my head slowly, as if I hadn't understood.

Soon after, she was gone, leaving scarcely a trace of herself, not a ripple on my life. Then a letter came from California. It read: "Who am I? Where are all my lesbian lovers? I wish you were here with a notebook. You could interview me about my childhood. I love you."

One night I went to Jilly's, a place I never go normally. It must have been obvious to all the women there that I didn't belong. I kept repeating to myself that I had a right to be there: I was looking for a missing piece in a puzzle. I walked by each table, looking at the women. Some smiled, one or two motioned me to sit down. With a smile I refused and kept looking, less and less hopeful. I walked all the way to the back, where the dancing was. Then I turned again and searched the tables one last time on my way out.

But Rose was not there.

Rebecca Brown

Isle of Skye

H ELLO IS EASY. IT'S THE SAME MOST PLACES. AND IF NOT, A SMILE OR A NOD will do. But then again, in some countries, a smile means sadness; and greeting is expressed with an open mouth shaped like the letter *O*.

I come to your house and drop my bag. Hello, I say.
Hello.
I wonder what the custom is, have I forgotten? You feed me tea and show me through your house. In both our countries, people sit on chairs. They walk on carpet or wood or cement or tile. They cover their walls with paper or paint. They put vases and mementoes on the mantels. Your house is different than I saw on my last visit.
In my country, you say, people live in homes.
That's like my country too.
So far so good.

You feed me tea. We talk about the miles and years between us. I pull out my Berlitz and smile, embarrassed when I have to look up your words. But you're patient with me and that's a good sign. I try to take my time and not to rush. Sometimes I look up a word you don't say, but just a word I'm thinking. I want to know how you'd think this feeling if you were thinking it yourself. Such as Desire, Longing, Want, Desire. I don't ask you.

The first time she left I knew she would not return. I was desolate. I did not want to remember her. I did not tell her. I forgot her. Which was possible because we'd never spoken. I had only my imagination to forget. She sent me postcards. She'd always travelled light. She returned suddenly and light. Carrying a Berlitz book and a passport. I was happy for the former. We sat down with it at once.

We try to talk and think we do, but we are each afraid. We know when we say blue that we mean blue. But maybe when you say blue, you mean sky. And maybe I mean water. Maybe we don't know to ask more than that. Maybe we don't know there's sky and chicory and Puget Sound. My eyes and navy uniforms. Maybe we don't know there's sapphire and moonstone and shower-wet slate, and that one shade from rain on oil. Maybe we don't know there's jay and powder, maybe we don't know skies. There are different coloured skies in Texas, Windermere, above the Isle of Skye. We have to know more to ask more. My country's colours are these: tall green dark timber from Oregon; shiny black hard coal, Ohio; bright red crisp apples, Oregon; thick black fat oil from Texas; red dirt from Oklahoma; bright blue lakes from Seattle. New Mexico is dusty brown; Arizona, blister white. I don't know yours.

We share an interest in foreign tongues, the languages you need when you're away. But you have never been abroad; I've always left my home. Maybe our interests are complements, exactly polar opposites. Or maybe they're just the same, two parts which once were intimate. We try hard to find out. We try to teach each other language.

I asked her where she'd been and where she was going. I knew that she was going. I pulled out the atlas from the bookshelf in my study. We sat on the carpet. She crouched down, kneeled on one leg, pulled the other leg up, she leaned over the two-page map and looked. She spaced both her palms out flat in the air and made a circle above the book.

It's a big place, she said. She looked at me and smiled. Then she pointed, I go here and then I go here. I watched her hand trace down the page. The distance looked so easy. I've got friends here, then I'll go back here. Her finger moved to its left. Then in a couple of days, I'll go back here. After that, here. I watched the shadow of her hand on the page, darkening the places. She tried to tell me about the smells of pine and salt and outdoor nights. Her fingers traced the routes that she had travelled. She said this map showed firm high mountains, deep cold lakes. But all I saw was a coloured page. She told me thick black knots were cities. I asked her to pronounce the names of cities where I've never been. She told me New York, Philadelphia, New Orleans. She said Seattle, Cincinnati, Portland. She said Dallas and Chicago. They sounded exotic. Did she try to make them so? The names were written in letters of different sizes. The route numbers were as big as other cities. The next page of the atlas showed a country they said was a tenth of the size of hers. The pictures were the same. This was my first lesson in the sorrow of our distance. I don't know if she knew.

We go for a walk so you can show me your country. We climb to the top of your favourite hill which you tell me has a view of your valley. They're long, low hills, yellow-brown and rubbed. They look tired and content. But it's foggy and we can't see anything beyond. You describe things that I must believe are there. I'd know more of a different thing if you'd show me a map. You say, When it's clear that's the Gloucester valley. There you can see to Malvern. There's a big outcrop of Cotswold stone and a cliff where people climb. We walk to the other side. Here you can see the Birdlip hill. Over there would be the Severn. There's a steeple

This kiss means this.

there that's tall and white and slim. I can't see anything. You pull me to you facing straight. Behind you fog is rolling. Your hair and lips are dark against the pale greying sky. Your voice is slow, deliberate, printing deep inside me. There's a rundown mill and a tiny stream and sheep are grazing below us. There's soft wet brilliant hummock grass and sheep with thick brown wool. Smoke is curling from the chimney at the pub. There's yellow stone homes and dogs and cars. There's wet thick tufts of green. There's soil and sky and cities. Your firm cold hands are on my shoulders. Your hair and lips are dark against the fog. You just have to believe me, you insist, *This is landscape.*

When I feel your palms against my back, I do. There's something like faith and something like light inside me. If you told me we were anywhere, we would be. I hope my words for "landscape," "fog," and "sky" are the same words in your language. I believe you.

We're sitting in your kitchen trading stories. In particular, your life story and my life story, the things that happened since my last visit to you. You ask me about my first lover and then my first love. I'm dying to confess. In broken phrases I explain, and hope you'll see my foundering as the struggle of a foreigner with language. I hesitate with my Berlitz, trying to avoid your eyes.

The difficulty, I decide, is just in language, the time it takes to find things in Berlitz. I know, I *know,* that in your country, as in mine, our needs come from our bodies. In your country, as in mine, surely your countrymen all need the same, to eat and sleep and love.

In this pause I look at you. Here's what I'll remember: your dark hair framing your brightened face, every shallow wrinkle near your mouth and eyes. Your cheek. I want a map of these soft creases. They look like tiny deltas. Your eyes are hard and soft like warm ice lakes, the ones you've said are three hours north of your home. Then there is one moment when your lips part slightly.

When you raise your hand to me, I hesitate. In my country, this means I want you. Should I search through my tour book, *The Ways and Customs of Your Country,* to find out what this means? But if I do I'll wreck the moment. Impulsively, I lunge. You pull me to you and when my mouth reaches yours, I think that I believe I understand you.

We give each other lessons, repeat phrases back and forth.
Blue is the sky above someplace.
Blue is the sky above someplace.
Desire is what you feel.
Desire is what you feel.
This kiss means this.
This kiss means this.
But no matter where we start, it's not back far enough. We can't explain "what you feel" or "this" or where is "someplace." We need to learn the first words first.

This kiss means this.

We try to get the basics. You explain mouth and thigh and knee to me. I define tongue and tooth and palm. You tell me what neck and breast and stomach mean. I say navel, leg and thigh. You give me the etymology of elbow and shoulder and back. I expound on fingers and flesh and thigh. You derive the roots of calf and rib. I trace back the sound of lip. You delineate the covert meaning of arm and ankle and wrist. I tell you mouth and breast and thigh. Every tongue is a foreign tongue. Your foreign tongue is mine.

This night we take each other to new countries neither of us has been to before. We are exhilarated, awed and lost. There are no maps.

I travel the cities from your knees to your thighs. My hands find avenues and lanes. This is a country road, a freeway, a round, smooth cobbled street. Your skin has deltas, soft like silt. The earth moves, is shattered, comes together again. I find I'm not a foreigner when my tongue finds the warmth between your thighs.

She refuses to be photographed, convinced she's not a tourist. She talks about rates of exchange, conversion factors, post. One of the little expenses too many travellers don't take into account, she says wisely, is what the bank will charge for their conversion. It's a hidden cost, she warns me. I don't listen.

One of our hands is on one of our thighs. One of our tongues is on one of our breasts. One of our hands is on one of our backs. One of our feet runs up one of our calves. One of our tongues is on one of our necks. One of our mouths is on one of our ears. One of our hands is in one of our thighs. One of us breathes and one of us breathes.

Both of us learn this means Yes.

Your back is straight and square and white. Your hands are smooth and tough. Your tongue is like an underwater plant. My hands begin to glow with sweet thick oil. Your eyes change colour. Your hands are smooth and tough.

We learn the meaning of the lack of sleep.

We make up words that we can't write or say, delicious, private, warm as thighs.

She's always travelled light and is proud of her travelling knowledge. She explains carefully how to pack her passport and her currency so pickpockets won't get at it. She keeps her passport by the bed, within reach of our lovemaking. Sometimes when she thinks I'm asleep, I hear her reach for it, run her fingertips on its old leather cover and sigh something I can't quite make out, I think another language.

We whisper syllables and touch. Our tongues touch and part, make words on fingertips, phrases from the tips of shoulders to chins, whole sentences and paragraphs on breasts. Pages on thighs. I think this time we forget what we know; that language is the only thing that lies.

This night we each wake from the same nightmare. Our stomachs are soaked in sweat.

Neither can remember the dream. When I wake up I lunge for the lamp and put us in the light. She grabs for her passport. The room looks bright and bare as a bulb.

Are you all right?

Are you?

I lean into her, my arms around her. We feel the sweat on one another's stomachs. She clutches her passport with one hand.

Hold me, I whisper. She tries.

I'm going to be ready, she says.

I'm afraid she is. I don't know where her pulse is racing.

Because in the dark when she's next to me, she whispers about transit. She says, It's like being in between. You could go anywhere.

I stroke her back and run my fingers down the soft bumps of her spine.

I say, But you aren't anywhere, are you? You're always in between.

She says, I like it right before you're there, when anything could happen. I don't ask if she's lost.

She speaks sentences from phrase books. In eleven languages she can ask when the next train leaves, is the water pure, where she can find a room. I know these phrases in only my own tongue, but many dialects, all rich.

You tell me, You are flexible, you're free. You wander many countries. You chat with all the natives. You move in and out of customs like a snake.

I protest, I say, You just don't know. This is the country I return to. I say, You are the country I return to. Insistent, I say, My home is not my home. You don't understand my freedom. All I have is papers. I tell you I am terrified of waking up in no man's land, my papers stolen, no one left to claim me or to understand my speech. My nightmare is that I'll be trapped without a phrase book or a tour guide, without a map to your land or to mine.

You say, But that is freedom.

I say, But that is fear.

The only way I can look is forward or back.

I keep coming back to you. Every time I leave, you say you know I won't return: I do. I come and come again to you. Each time I bring you more folk songs and tales from abroad. I think that's what you want from me. When will you believe I want to come back? When will you believe I would stay?

You tell me "stay" means something different in your land. It's not a simple cut and dried translation.

Sadly, wisely, we avoid all talk of idioms. We do not mention syntax or semantics. We don't talk about variant readings, hidden meanings or the foggy subtleties of pun. We avoid the meanings of double entendres. Because we know, though we try desperately to deceive ourselves, that it *is* a matter of semantics. The language that we know means something real. We pretend we only know what we say. Language is the only thing that lies.

I'm afraid I think that what you want are my amusing stories from abroad. The next time I come back, I'll bring a slide projector, a carousel, some books, a pile of pamphlets, a stack of postcards for the fridge. I'll show you packs and packs of photos, some rare exotic artifacts, and I'll talk about the habits of the natives. I'll bring you a goat from South America, a camel from the desert. I'll bring you a rickshaw and a pocket of pearls and a shell from Bora Bora. I want to present these things to you, to lay them on the mantelpiece. I want you to keep them. I'll become a curiosity, exaggerate my mannerisms. I'll be a parody to charm you. When will you believe these words and maps, these anecdotes are what I give, the way I'm trying to ask you, let me stay?

This is not what sustains her here. To keep her I must send her out. She is not happy still. There are ways she is that here would be a fool. We know the ways that we could not survive. Loving difference causes pain. We love what is different to possess it, to be whole. We want to be everything. The problem is, we can't. The problem is, the differences are different. Water and flame, brilliance and night, longing and fulfilment of desire. What keeps us moving is what keeps us sad, what keeps us moving is the want to be unforeign, whole.

Some words we try to translate just don't work. We can't agree. What you see as my freedom, I call fear. What I name strength in you, you label fear. I have to remind you of the beautiful cadences in your speech, the way your phrases fall like tides and rain and fog. You tell me mine are like lightning and like fog. Neither of us believes the other.

Will I get homesick or the travel itch? Will you get tired of being patient with my lack of fluency in your language? Your lessons with me cut into your life. You'll wonder, is the payoff worth the effort?

You insist that I'd get bored; you're right. You tell me you'd get irritated; you're right. The fact is, we are different. Our union is a sharp specific point, the few words we've translated, the tiny border crossed.

I want to make true promises. I want to say when I'll be back. You hand me my passport, give me my worn Berlitz, and take me to the station.

In the train station, we stand apart, our bodies puzzled by distance. When I reach to hold you goodbye all our words rush up and out of me. I've forgotten how to speak. I touch your lips. I know this is a custom, is it yours or mine? Do you know what it means? Through the greasy yellow window on the train, I see you. You're leaning against a post and you are smiling. Your lips are mouthing words that I can't understand. I try to focus but I can't see. Are you trying to say you love me or goodbye? I start to raise my hand to you, then the train jolts. Did you see what I meant to do? Do you know this means I love you? Do you know this means I love you?

I take a train and then another train and then a bus and then a plane. I catch another bus, a cab, a train. I try to backtrack, circle back. I'm trying to throw something off my trail. Because I want a miracle. I want you to find me. I keep looking back, in rearview mirrors, over my shoulder, through fog.

At borders they check my passport, crumpled, stamped with my history. The nation of my origin is blurred, buried under coloured marks of countries I've forgotten. And of yours.

At customs I declare these goods: three nights of love, a champagne cork, a picture in a garden. Two walks, a four-day conversation, memories of hands. The scent of our flesh on my clothes, a memory of red. Some syllables that I can't spell, the tension in your thighs. The feel of hands, a sound of breath, the texture of your skin above your eyes. The magic feel of twice blessed flesh. The cold grey light of morning on your spine.

In this newly foreign country I've called home, my countrymen look different. I've forgotten how to say hello. I wake up at the wrong time, suffering jet lag.

I dream sadly and with longing of our transport. I long for you, I long for when we shall pass free through one another's homes. But this is a dream from which I awake.

I wake as if I were with you. I leave this narrow bed and walk streets I remember only dimly. I try to read the road signs and recall my native language, my own tongue.

In your land, it is morning. You're making tea and going out to work. I wander the darkened foggy streets alone, pretending in the dark half-light I'll see you. The sky here now is foggy orange, the false light of the streetlamps.

I'm lost in a city whose name you can't pronounce; I think it is my own. Your country's maps spell this name differently. Will you recognize the postmark? Will you recognize my hand? Who'll translate the maps for us? Do you know this means I love you? Do you

Ramabai Espinet

Erotic Fragments

In and out of the city where I live

THE EDGES OF THE STORM HOLD NO SURPRISES FOR ME—NEVER DID. I HAVE lived underneath those edges from time begun so far off that now I forget. And remember only thin dreams of dawns that start in a place of white water, sand and a cock-crowing morning colder and fresher than apple crunch and sea-spray ... only thin dreams of what was ... once upon a time.

Spring in the city where I live. At the bottom of the street, two hairdressing shops stand side by side: Mena's and Fortunato's. She does ladies' hair, he looks after men. A pocket-handkerchief partnership. The street is wonderful: half-dirty, tall trees above, apple and cherry blossoms and rambling rosebushes running on trellises, tight-assed little yards, people hustling to make it, to make something. An ordinary city street ... My life is rooted here in a daily happiness. I hole myself up in my attic and work like a demon. At night I take walks. Early in the morning I sit at the window and stare at trees.

Love in this city has not found me. I journey from this side of my city street to see my lover where he sits, inside of Babylon itself, taking too many drugs and playing too much hard bright music. He is warm, beautiful, comforting. We huddle in his tiny flat on the four-teenth floor, drink martinis the first day out of cracked clay tumblers, drink rum the second day, cheap wine the next. His skin is rosy black, with the deep purple of eddoes; his mouth tastes of rum and the charge of approaching sex, night, jewels, stars.

Our lovemaking is rock and sand and water, he sucks and bites my breasts until I am half-dead from delight and fear of what will happen next, such is love, such should be love for-ever. When he enters me the first day he is as large as trees and forests, and I shake so much he has to stop—it has been a long time. His largeness gives me rain and stars, the strength in his leg muscles, his waist, rivet me to a place I never want to come back from ... I reach for more, and more ...

The incredible shape of a man's body. His arms, the muscles in his shoulders ... In the park, under the roughness of a red and gold plaid blanket we make love quietly. No one else lives in this place but us, hidden under a mess of shrubbery, somewhere in the back of tall trees. He props himself up on one elbow and looks at my face. What is so incredible about his beauty at this exact moment? Maybe the red-black glow underneath his dark skin or his eyelashes curling downwards or his face grown taut with desire. For me.

Going to a club to hear jazz, walking for hours, stopping for ice-cream cones, holding hands. On Sunday morning a shaft of sunlight falls across his pillow cutting a gold panel through that purple-black caimite skin. I wake him up, and he kisses my un-mouthwashed jungle mouth. A series of small spaces forms a latticed pattern between our making love and sleeping ... Will this ever end? It mustn't.

Yet all the while I know that forever can be just one day, or two or three. Divided by drugs, by life, by distance, we meet anyhow in an arc spun high above the city, slung low inside of this tenement in Harlem where he lives, running for dear life towards a space that must swallow him up as quickly as it can. I run towards it too. But more slowly.

Safe sex?

So what does fucking consist of really? Different things with different people. The way that friendships, conversations, a night out on the town, maybe, mean different things with different people. A journey in which memory holds no details, and only the flow into a place of rock and water is left. Of a game some play where he, my lover, tries to have it all and preserve all his safe anchors. When this happens I swear a madness flies into my head and all my thought is focused upon wrecking that pitiful little latch onto his safe domestic anchorage. No malice intended, only pure cussed instinct, my love.

Like with the successful corporate type whom I drove at two a.m. to a house in the country. Tearing through the streets of Port-of-Spain, old Caribbean city, dogs barking, streetlights off (or on at random, and me speeding into oblivion). The lighthouse, the vendors sleeping at the side of the road with their produce, the cart of ice-cold coconuts, women selling shark and bake and roti, tearing past the everyday signposts of city streets to a place of absolute sex, maybe? Him saying weakly, God how you've got my adrenalin going, God I've got to have you. And so you shall, so you shall, me ironical for no good reason.

Yet in bed adventurously crawling all over my body, fingers, arms, toes, tongue, his cock on my forehead, in my ear, my cunt tracing stars everywhere on his body from nose to the knobbly fronts of beautiful knees, he finds the time to whisper just before he makes me come for the first of a dozen times, it seems, don't, don't scratch my back.

My nails are slightly long, defensively, I guess. Did I think of scratching his back before he issued this condition? I don't know. But he says this and my hands curl of their own accord. I don't do it right away. We make love for hours, and I forget about it. But some time in the night my nails move on their own and rake his back, the insides of his wonderful legs, down across his neck and chest. He leaves me unmarked.

He wants safety, and I want him to have it. But not this time. He is a beautiful, sincere, longing kind of man. Any woman could sleep with a man like that all night long. So can his wife, I'm sure. I've learnt that it's the journey into sleep that matters; the lovemaking part is easy, but you can't sleep with everyone. We sleep upside down in the end. When did we move to breathe deeply into each other's faces, mouths, eyes … some time deep in the heart of sleep … I don't know. We wake up early and together, discovering that we are holding hands.

So was he safe? Was I? Bodily fluids were exchanged, pain, grief, scars of love exchanged. The antiseptic barricades torn to the ground … If I live, if I die, what does it matter anyhow? Leh me dead, man, leh me dead …

Carambolas

Ba-a-a-ad, unrepressed sexuality. Or pleasure maybe. Not confined to closed, stale rooms, small spaces, hot air, stifled moans, week-old sheets. Another kind altogether: high windowless rooms, a breeze from the sea, a man's brown iron arm, a sea-breath, a laugh, a song. Not sometimes. Always. A fearless merging with another—without distance—without drawing fucking breath …

Only this day counts

We wake up to the sound of police sirens as is usual in his neighbourhood. Up on the eleventh floor high off the street stretching and yawning and flexing in bed before the day announces itself.

What shall we do with a day so perfect, a time so right that stooping to pick up stars from the grass down below seems more natural than coffee and morning sounds? When I knew I loved you that way it seemed better to lie down and die than to let those feelings grow into ordinariness.

Moving to the rhythm deep inside his waist, licking and sucking, caressing underneath his armpits, the backs of his knees, his arse, biting his nipples, wondering where this series of movements into love will go today on its way into the melting fuck that waits for us.

The times before, other men whom I've loved and longed for … everything becomes a haze into which I travel in and out … all part of the same movement.

He gets up and goes to the bathroom. I listen to him peeing, listen to him going to the kitchen, bringing back coffee to the bed, going back out for the newspaper, bringing all of it back to the bed. His movements are certain, deadly, extraordinary. His face gold, his eyes brown, his cheekbones cutting a wedge underneath the laugh lines in his face, his eyebrows forever on the brink of surging upwards into ironical disbelief … I want him so much.

He is a man who has entered my body and my life entirely uninvited, at least so my rational self believes. My other live, subversive self has no thought of anything but this moment of madness and magic. I want, I must, it's right, take it and run with it, it's maybe forever and maybe today but who the fuck cares? And so what in the end? Take it and run with it, it's good, it's great, it's yours.

He is a man who has entered my body and my life with a vastness of desire that I had forgotten. Its vastness burns a hole in my inattention to desire, consumed by work, by life as I am. It burns whole acreages of resistance to desire down to the ground.

Desire … resistance … made to walk, not run, through rooms grown ancient by indifference, forcing me into want. I want, I want, more than wind and water and freedom.

Today I'm a big woman. A big woman fully alive in my body. A big woman born out of the Caribbean Sea. It takes time to reach this place. My friend Kadiran says when asked about her single life, when I want a man I just take one. I don't want one for keeps. Which woman needs that? I think so too a lot of the time.

But not this time. I want to meet him, know him. Know him carnally so I can really know him. Now I know that carnal knowledge IS knowledge. Vast and unterritorialized.

Later in the day, going down in the elevator, there is a magical quietness in the air. We stand side by side, close together. On the seventh floor a stranger gets in and stands at a diagonal, in the opposite corner. We instinctively ease away and move closer together. Then, with the lightest of moves he jams me, my lover, into the corner of the elevator and leans against me, pressing hard. A small movement really, a small movement generating the incredible thrill of being pressed by a man you desire beyond moon and rain and forever against the corner of an elevator while he leans against you, purely male, purely human, purely him as he was meant to be.

Safe, warm, comfortable. Dangerous, risky, perched on a ledge. At the same time. Don't bring me back from this into ordinariness. The only thing I want to do with you my love is to fall right off the fucking cliff. Make me fall over, make me, I want to fall over the fucking edge … Who cares about what lies down below? Ordinariness can wait for tomorrow, today, only this day counts.

Cassie Jameson
Not Your Bitch

IN ALL THE THOUSANDS OF MILLIONS OF YEARS THAT MEN AND WOMEN HAVE co-existed on this planet, one thing remains constant: women have always been the oppressed. After reading one of the oh-so-detailed paragraphs that occur so frequently in my history book about our treatment over the centuries, I'm left wondering how could they take that shit? Then, why do we still take shit? Textbooks are only one example. There are children being taught out of a book that devotes a half-page to Alexander Hamilton's hair-do and a paragraph every several chapters to women's roles in society. As if this wasn't insulting enough, they then go on to explain how even though only property-owning white males were allowed to vote, women still had plenty of influence through their husbands. I can't believe someone living in this century wrote that. It's time to stop living through our husbands/boyfriends and start behaving like the pissed-off females we are! Whenever I think about the chicks I know that change completely with each new boyfriend, I feel the urge to spew burrito chunks. I have a hard time respecting anyone who can't respect themselves enough to remain an individual, or thinks it necessary to adapt to someone else's "scene". Homegirl please, get a job. Don't misunderstand, I'm not saying change is bad, change is what makes you grow, but change for yourself, not for someone else. Men have told us what we should look like and what's "acceptable" for us to do for a millennium too long. I'm not saying declare all men pigs, just the ones that scream "hey baby" out the windows of their four-by-fours, or those that happen to accidentally misplace their hands on your breast. Though screaming "don't touch my breast" (Kim Gordon, "Swimsuit Issue") to sexual harassers is a big step, we shouldn't stop there. What I'm babbling about is it bums me out that I can't think of any local chick bands. Call me crazy but I don't think this is due to lack of talent. The oppression won't stop until everyone knows how we feel. By no means does music have to be the only form of communication; for those of us less-coordinated gals (myself not excluded), screaming, yelling and kicking things work just as well. As long as you make a scene and get your point across. So call yourself a Riot Grrrl and start making as many scenes as you deem necessary to be understood. Realize you are a rad female because you are not the image this male-dominated society wants you to be. You don't owe anyone but yourself anything. So fight like a girl and take no shit!

G-POWER!

Lisa Sakulensky

Toronto 1986

Paris 1991

Evelyn Lau

Mercy

I T IS YOUR WIFE'S FORTIETH BIRTHDAY AND I AM TORTURING YOU TO THE SOUNDS of a tape of Dylan Thomas giving a poetry reading. His voice is theatrical and at times it hovers at the edges of breaking into song. "Do not go gently into that good night ... Rage, rage against the dying of the light ...." His words, charged with command, seem to pulse through my own body. Obediently I slip the spiked heel of my shoe into your mouth. You are watching me with confusion because I am drunk and balancing over your naked body takes more skill than you think. I don't want to fall on you with my weight and the stabbing silver of my bracelet, injuring you, making it impossible for you to meet your wife later in the evening for dinner down by the harbour where the white ships come in. She will chatter on about *The New York Review of Books*, literary magazines, publishers' conventions and other things that bewilder you because you decided to make money in medicine instead of writing poetry. Neither of us knew when we made our respective choices that we might be equally unfulfilled. I do not want to hurt you, at least not clumsily, not out of drunkenness, not because the high arches of my feet prevent me from balancing in spike heels. I want it to mean something when I hurt you, I want each transgression to be a deliberate one that cuts both ways, something that neither of us will be able to blame on bottles of wine or the fact that when I am in this position, one foot balanced on your neck, there is nothing nearby to hold on to and the only thing stable is the floor which seems a long way off from up here.

I will not go gentle into you. The high heel of my shoe is in your mouth and it is cutting the roof where the flesh is ridged and ticklish. You suck the heel like you would a phallus and I wonder what you are tasting, what grotty remains of dust and dirt and sidewalk you are swallowing down the soft pinkness of your throat. Up here I can see you are going bald, the expanse of your forehead with your grey hair tossed backwards onto the carpet is wide and gleaming. With your eyes shut and your mouth working to please the point of my shoe, you could easily be an inflatable doll or a cartoon and I am able then to withdraw my heel as carefully as a penis and rake it in pink crescents across your cheek and down your chin.

In my sessions with you I search for the evil inside us that we share like kisses between our open mouths. The boundaries I once saw as steel fences in my mind turned out to be sodden wooden planks when I reached them, easily kicked down. Each act of pain became easier to inflict once the initial transgressions had been committed, and we had understood ourselves capable of surviving them. Once I even tried on myself the things I do to you. Whipping myself with a silver chain, I became fascinated by the stopped seconds of pain that opened my mouth and closed my eyes. Afterwards I was left looking down at the thighs where the circle of the chain I had snapped down my body had left a perfect imprint of itself, pink like a rubber stamp, like one of those playful rubber stamps with happy faces on them.

When the pain stopped, time moved again and I wondered if perhaps in our time together you felt this also, this stopping of time as it races past you now that you are middle-aged and some of your friends are already dead. Perhaps only the absorption of pain can distract you from the details of your daily life—the necessary hours at the office, the teenaged children demanding money for concerts and clothes, the golf lessons on weekend afternoons. All this leading you down the road of increasing age, minor illnesses and death.

"Old age should burn and rave at close of day," Thomas instructs sternly. Perhaps only in the clutches of pain, when your eyes are closed and your lips forced apart, does the day seem long. Perhaps this is what you seek, this element of immortality, the way I do by writing poems. I tried that day to understand what it must be like for you when the pain hits, when you protest with a convulsion in your voice that stops me because it is no longer pleasurable pleading that runs out of your mouth like water or thin blood.

It is easy to become addicted to hurting you, to aching for that moment when you take off your clothes and lie on my floor. There is a slight roundness to your stomach and a soft field of black chest-hair that sharpens into a tiger's stripe running down your belly. It appears knife-like, sadistic. I could picture you with a black beard, trying on black leather vests and turning in a mirror like the men I watch downtown in the shops I frequent now, fascinated, struck by how warmly this fringe community welcomes me. I had never before been accepted so unquestioningly elsewhere. I finger the bewildering chains of my new trade and talk to the women behind the counter who are pierced and smiling and who recommend books that make me realize I am only on the circumference and that the centre has no bottom. You could just as easily have been one of those men who advertise for young blond slaves to torture, who read magazines that teach them how to build benches and restraints and instruments of pain. You could have turned like that and I am given to understand that perhaps one afternoon you will. Some nights I pace my apartment and wonder if one day I will push you too far and you will break like that. There is no way either of us can tell, because we are each other and there is nothing restraining that moment when we exchange power like others do body fluids.

SLAP

The power floods into me warm and soft and golden, dusty as pollen. I had not realized previously the extent of my emptiness that no kisses could fill, no flowers or brave

PINCH

words of love. The emptiness sang hollow and blue and then turned red as rage. I knew from the first session that I could have killed you and that indeed you were not letting me go so far as I needed. Looking down at your muscled body on my floor, I wanted some of that red inside me to bleed out through you, in slashes and strokes of thudding colour.

You bought me a bracelet the other day from one of the sex shops downtown. It was sitting curled up in a dusty corner of the glass case, half-concealed by wrinkly dildoes and packets of Day-Glo creams and lotions. I was browsing impatiently, needing to use the bathroom, my feet swelling in my heels, bored by the plastic-coated magazines and multi-coloured underwear nailed to the walls. The woman behind the counter had a toothless glazed expression and eyes that looked like they were made of glass. I did not particularly want to be there and perhaps neither did you, you were lifting your watch every so often to check the time and thinking of dinner with your wife who if you were lucky might wear the red leather outfit you bought her, even if she never assumed the role. There was no time that afternoon to duck into changing rooms with burgundy lace and ripped, fringed leather skirts. The fluff no longer interested me, the delicacy of lingerie seemed an offence. It was the trickling cat o' nine tails that tickled my fingers, it was the canes perched rigid on the walls, it was even that morbid black leather mask moulded to the dummy's unseeing white face on the top counter that ran currents through me. I felt as though the world I had walked on for years had flipped and on the other side there lived people who turned up palms of blood and leather.

The woman with the motionless eyes uncurled the bracelet and we felt the tips of the studs. When she said the bracelet had been banned I said I wanted it and you paid for it and that night I fell asleep with it on my wrist while candles flickered around the room in crystal holders. It tormented me all night because each time I moved my hand I would hurt myself into consciousness. The next day I wore it and pretended it was a joke from a friend, and at lunch a man came to my table and said, You could kill somebody with that. His eyes were brown and overly trusting. Later when I hugged my lunch companion goodbye she let out a yelp and said, You stabbed me in the back.

BITE

It will be a good toy for next time, applied to the more vulnerable parts of your body. I will stroke you with the eager points of the bracelet and then I will hurt you with them. That is part of the joy, the caresses that I allow before pressing down the pain. I like it best when I kiss you with full-mouthed tenderness before slapping your face, when I lick a finger and circle it lightly around the head of your penis, before pinching the skin of the shaft, when I take one of your truncated nipples into my mouth and stroke its little hard point between my teeth before I bite.

I listen to you when you call at night needing somebody to talk to and I spend half an hour with you on the phone while you talk about your marriage and your kids and your practice and I never tell you you are boring me or that my time is not for you. I show my harmlessness by giving you books of poetry, but I am never able to read more than a few lines aloud to you before you become impatient and pull me to the floor, where we lose our words and our regular faces.

If we are victims of each other, then in those moments we are the most beautiful victims in the world. Sometimes when I stand over you, when my heels are gouging into you, I look beyond you towards some thin line of distance and understand that each time your face wrenches with pain I am spreading a slow dark stain down the still-white years of my future, and that in that sense you are killing me and not the other way around. Each time you scream it wrings out the light in me and leaves twisted red and black cords like knotted whips lying on the wall and waiting, hungering to be used, to be applied against white skin that flinches away and cries.

You have the kind of engaging smile and blue eyes that, in the daytime, make you one of the most popular dentists in the city. How could your patients know those same fingers take a piece of wire and wind it so tightly around the base of your penis that I wince for you? How could they know your mouth fills with everything that sifts across the bottom of high-heeled shoes that have walked the pavement? You are friendly enough, your hand cups their trusting chins, you see into them and reassure them. You see into them the way you saw into me the first night we met over drinks and lounge music, and even though I said little and at that time knew nothing, you saw something in me you described as dark, very dark, you saw a part of me I had not seen in hours of mirror reflections.

This is not a game, you kept saying until I heard it every night in my dreams. You can call it a game if you like, but I will do almost anything you want, whatever that might be.

I thought that would translate into walks on the beach and poetry readings and drinking wine, that those would be the extent of my desires. I did not expect this rage that continues to grow rather than subside as you plead with me now to stop, as a thin growl rises in my throat and razors the air.

It is your wife's fortieth birthday and Dylan Thomas's voice slows to a stop on the tape. You edge out the door with the sun bouncing off your glasses and your briefcase tucked under your arm. It is always remarkable to me, these partings, how we are able to assume again the responsibilities of work and life as though nothing had changed, as though we had not been permanently altered by our actions. On the surface things are as they always have been—you are discreet with your sounds; no one asks questions. I sit down at the typewriter and rub my swollen feet, their chafed heels, thinking of our obligations toward wives and poetry and thinking that perhaps this is just as well, we do not want the end to come too soon, the irreversible outcome of the final scene. We want to taste our pleasure bit by bit, inch by inch, we want to lick it slowly and make it last, we will make it good and make it last, my poor tiger-striped victim, we will make ourselves into people we hate enough to kill.

Dawn Mourning

Her Needs

Some days she's so horny,
she could attack the first cock
she meets on the street.
It's like the world is centred
just above her knees.
Cream on
a woman in need.

Most days she's not indifferent
to the attentions of men.
She flatters and flirts
or carefully eludes.
Like close fitting jeans
it drives them mad,
a tight squeeze.

Some days she doesn't give a fuck
then she has to beat them
off with a stick.
Indifference being
a strong attraction,
she rubs it in;
a cock tease.

Some days when she's had a good lover

she's so pleased,
she could kiss every man she meets.
It's like the world is focused
between her knees.
Creamed jeans
a woman freed.

The Italian Lover

The Italian lover
makes love with his voice
when making love …

"Bitch
You beautiful bitch
Do it how I like it
Do it like I say
Do it real nice
Please
Only you know how to do it
Oh Baby
I love your ass
Your breasts
Those beautiful breasts
Suck me, Baby
Do it right
Or I'll bite
I'll eat you
I'll do it the way you like
Do you want it?
Here, take me
Up your ass
Your beautiful ass
I'll hurt you
Up front
Up your cunt
Up your hot cunt
Bella
Bene
Exquisimo-o-o-o"

Right Lane Lemons

The romance was conducted in the produce department of the supermarket. As he stacked bright River King oranges, she draped her body against a basket of Red Delicious apples, inviting him on. Like the tiny yellow pits of the Right Lane lemons, all was revealed under fluorescent lights. Erotic fantasies lay bared beside the neat rows of Head Man's lettuce. He placed deep green cucumbers and told of his need for a demanding woman. She declared her want of a virile man as he deftly handled Dear One grapefruit. Two passions begging to be released like the juices of ripe Bartlett pears. They crossed wits over tapering soft green celery and laughed at suggestively posed Dole bananas. Their eyes interlocked and said all. Senses attuned, their imaginations clung together like a bunch of Jasmine Vineyard green grapes. They fell into each other and devoured.

What did the customers say as they selected I'm Asleep radishes and Blue Bird pomegranates? Nothing! The feast of pleasure was as unnoticeable as the tiny yellow pits on the Right Lane lemons.

Backdoor Man

You wanted a secret
to hold so close
that it licked
the base of your balls.
So you've got it.
A secret
to wrap round yourself
late at night
and grin at.
Cherish it.
Carry it deep inside
preferably from behind.
Keep the mystery
of your glistening black buttocks
against perfect half moons
close to your heart.
Away from the prying truth
of your own private need,
crouched on top

in the clandestine position.
That secret.
The sweet scent of sweat
lingering on past
the slippery breasts
and crumpled black sheets.
Relish it.
The wet memory
of swollen parts
early in the morning,
and hold it dear.
Because a secret
is all you've got.

The Cry of a Frustrated Woman

The cry of a frustrated woman
to a gentleman:

"Don't just stand there,
take me.
Throw me down
and fuck me.
You've got a cock
use it,
for something more than pissing.
You've got strength
show it,
do something more than kissing.
You're a man
prove it,
take what you need
give what I want."

Mary Gaitskill
The Rose Taboo

THERE WAS A PICTURE OF AXL ROSE IN A MAGAZINE RECENTLY. THE ARTICLE was about an L.A. pleasure palace where empty, beautiful people—those bastards!—come to shake their booties and girls get in by showing their implants to the doorman. Axl was only mentioned once in the piece, but the picture was perfect. Bloated, bleary, grinning a grin of bewildered entitlement as he pulled up the dress of a clinging girl to show the gorgeous ass upon which he had just written his name, the Axl in the photo was a vector for fantasies of fascination and resentment, a template of full-throttle bawling and bellowing, grabbing and eating. "Really revolting," commented the person who showed me the picture. That's how you're supposed to react, but I don't know ... If I was a twenty-nine-year-old rock star and I was bombed out of my skull and a beautiful girl came and wiped herself on me, I'd write my name on her ass, too.

Axl (more accurately, Axl's public image; I've not met the flesh-and-blood man) reminds me of a kid I knew in junior high school, a small, pouty, gum-chewing androgynous brat named Brad. Brad was also someone I had secret empathy for, even though I thought I shouldn't. In a desolate landscape of square brick houses on square sod lawns, one stunted tree per lawn, he proudly slouched and sneered and snot-balled his way through life, wild and sensually cruel, yet stiffly adhering to complex social rules that I, to my dismay, could make no sense of. He wasn't a loner; there were lots of kids like him, and I was scared of them for their wildness and their conformity, both of which seemed to burst from the constricted environment with alarming force.

But I also admired these kids for their beauty, their audacity and panache. I was fascinated by the cruelty that ran through all their discourse like blood. Brad in particular was clever and maddeningly cute; his vicious taunting of the wretched special-ed student had the exquisite refinement of a hot needle. I thought it was wrong and it made me sick, but in its extremity it had a horrible intensity that, just in terms of sheer wattage, was stronger than anything else I saw in our sadly bland environment. And teenagers, even quiet, shy ones, need and love intensity; they'll take it where they can find it.

This is what Guns N' Roses music, especially as put across by Axl Rose, is about. Not cruelty specifically, but rather the kind of boundless aggression that can easily turn to cruelty. It is intense and generically fierce—generic because it doesn't have to be directed at anybody or anything in particular, whether Rose intends it to be or not. Some critics like to talk about how "dangerous" or "on the edge" the band are, citing their drug and alcohol excesses as if their music is the result of their being really "out there". This is a bunch of shit. It doesn't matter if their nastiness and fierceness is justified by their touted "street" experiences or not. An elementary-school kid who's been shoved out of the lunch line knows where Axl's furious screams are coming from. A tiny old lady hobbling down the street knows. *All* human beings know, on some level, of those moments when you want to stick your hand up somebody's ass and tear his guts out. To hear that fly out of the radio, streamlined by Axl's high, carnal, glandularly defined voice, is an invitation to step into an electrical stream of pure aggression and step out again. This opportunity to connect, even indirectly, with an experience of realized power is going to be a seductive sensation for anybody. For people who don't acknowledge this aggression and violence in themselves, it is either irresistibly compelling or very frightening or both—like Brad's appalling meanness was for me. And Axl's aggressiveness can be appallingly mean to easy targets—you know, "faggots," "niggers," "bitches," etc.

I have a male friend who confessed to me, with a certain guilt and embarrassment, that once, while sitting alone in a sushi bar reading about a highly publicized rape trial, his disgust and anger about the rape somehow turned into arousal, and he had to head for the bathroom to beat off. He said part of it was the flat, matter-of-fact journalese with which the violence and obscenity were described; other than that he didn't rationally understand why something that he considered brutal and grossly unjust (the rapists were acquitted) affected him this way. I think he expected me to hate him, but I didn't. For one thing, you can't legislate your sexual fantasies, and it doesn't do much good to suppress them. More important, fantasy is not reality. This person would never rape anyone (in fact, when he was a juror in a rape trial, he successfully persuaded an ambivalent jury to convict). People's fantasies are much like dreams in that they are not strictly literal; dream and fantasy images often have a more complex meaning than is immediately apparent. Besides, aggression and sex are both inherently arousing in different ways. Put them together and you can get something strong enough to smash a fist through all your rational defences. This is the level that GNR is operating on, except that it is something that everybody, including women, can dip into and experience at whatever depth they want. And nobody gets raped.

Some critics would hurl their *History of Rock, Vol. 1* at me at this point and argue that women are figuratively raped by Axl's misogynist lyrics. At least one critic I've read commented that he thought Axl's female fans lacked self-respect. I understand why he might feel this way, but I don't agree. There is great ferocity latent in women—latent because culturally we still don't support or acknowledge it. My fascination with little Brad was partly, in retrospect, a result of a disavowal of my own aggression and meanness. If I couldn't see it in myself, I had to fixate on it in someone else, in an exaggerated form. If I'd been able to acknowledge it and take responsibility for my own like qualities, I wouldn't have had to create this polarized situation where he was on one end being mean and I was on the other end being nice. My fascination with him was, at its murky bottom, a desire to connect with something in myself and bring it into balance. Similarly, I imagine that girls, even more so than boys, could look at Axl Rose and feel intense delight at seeing him embody their unexpressed ferocity, and thus experience it temporarily through him. This is an attempt at integration on a gut level and makes the kind of "self-respect" referred to by the critic look like a rag.

The niggers/faggots stuff is different. I don't blame blacks or gays who have a problem with Axl Rose. But song lyrics are like short stories; at best they are full renderings of an emotional or experiential state, not statements of how life should be lived or how the writer feels for all time. I once had an argument with a lesbian friend over Axl Rose, during which I asked her if she ever felt like just saying "Get out of my way" to anybody and everybody. Queer Nation and ACT UP sure have. If you like the "fuck you" part of a song, then you take it into yourself and let it help you tell people to fuck off; the "who" part is your choice, not the singer's. Who Axl really hates or doesn't hate is his problem and should be given no power.

There are lots of bands that equal or surpass GNR in intensity and aggression, but most of them are nowhere near as big. What gets GNR over is their mainstream and essentially suburban sensibility. (Coming from me, that's not an insult. *My* sensibility is in large part suburban.) Some smaller, grungier bands work out of a suburban sensibility—but they give its generality a convulsive aesthetic specificity. Axl, on the other hand, goes straight out and down the centre. Take the *Paradise City* video. Its most salient features: huge mobs o' people, big spaces, big noises, bigness period. Come one, come all. The *Paradise* crowd scenes are an amorphous, mobile, boundless universe that is accessible and ordinary, yet blown up into an ordinariness of monstrous proportions. Nubile groupies pout while boyishly gloating Axl displays a backstage pass reading ACCESS ALL AREAS—nudge, wink—his ridiculous expression of self-indulgence mitigated by an undertone of ingenuous vulgarity that is oddly sweet. (I imagine he had the same look on his face when he made his absurdly banal I-love-lesbians comment to *Rolling Stone*.) It's the democracy of porn; you don't have to be hip or possess arcane sensibility to understand where Axl is coming from. But unlike many other mainstream bands, the sexiness doesn't deteriorate into softness or silliness because it's consistently laminated to fluxtuating, boundless fierceness. Lots of male performers gyrate their hips. But when Axl does it the way he does it in, say, *Welcome to the Jungle*, it's not just his hips. His rapt, mean little face, the whole turgor of his body, suggests a descent into a pit of gorgeous carnal grossness, a voluptuousness of awful completeness where, yes, "you're gonna die."

If this sounds like a hormonal response, that's because it is. Axl is obviously sexy. But the reasons go beyond hormonal button-pushing. When I look at him I feel a lot like I'm looking at that little snot Brad again. Only this time I'm not scared. This time I want to embrace him. By "embrace" I don't mean it's O.K. to be a rude prick and hate queers. Nor do I mean I want to find Axl and rip his clothes off. I mean I want to make peace with all the elements of myself, and if getting off on Axl helps me do that, so be it.

In a recent interview with *Rolling Stone*, Axl joined the ranks of those confessing their childhood abuse. With Roseanne Arnold it may have been soul murder, with Axl it's "My dad fucked me in the ass when I was two." Ai yi yi. According to some people, this means Axl "just wants to be a victim". Maybe. I would guess not, though. My sense is that Axl has reflexively absorbed the current mood of helplessness with the ingenuous and enthusiastic vulgarity he displays elsewhere. He penetrates society in a big way, and it penetrates him back. Actually, it's believable to me that he was abused or at least ignored. When I was young, the mean high-school kids I knew looked like inexplicable, cruel monsters. Now I think their wildness and aggression were part of their fierce teenage spirit—which, as I said, didn't have much room to move in its bland environment. When youthful ferocity is ignored and not given real guidance, it can turn vicious and ugly. In this respect, Axl's public persona is an amplification of an angry boy who has never been taught to develop his intensity and power into maturity, who is therefore wildly flailing about, locked in an endless drama of compulsive aggression that can never be satisfied. My strong reaction to him is in part an impulse to make it better, for him as well as for me.

Once, I dreamed about Axl. In the dream we were on an airplane flying somewhere. We weren't particularly happy to be sitting together, but it was a long flight and we both fell asleep. When I woke up, we had our arms around each other, not erotically but companionably. When we saw what we were doing, we jerked apart and regarded each other warily. We resumed our forward-facing travelling postures, our body language subtly changed by the realization that we'd touched and survived. Maybe next dream I'll get to write my name on his ass.

Pamela Des Barres

The Dirty Minds in '69

I

I WAS BACKSTAGE WITH THE DIRTY MINDS, FEIGNING HIPNESS, MY HEART HEAVING out of my Pocohontas mini-dress, when Mr. Faith finally appeared, his hair in perfect ebony tangles. Grabbing a bottle of Jack Daniels with one hand and my ass with the other, he grinned "C'mon, luv, let's brave the mob." The security guards staved off the natives; flashbulbs popped, girls wailed, journalists waved their pencils, and I was right in the middle of a minefield, rows of envious eyes boring holes into my concocted nonchalance. Davy held my hand hard and tight as we headed for the car. The big roadie, whose name turned out to be Clive, led the way like a grizzly bear in battle, and in seconds we were ensconced within the Cadillac womb. Plush luxury, sweet-smelling soft leather seats, an oak bar chock-a-block with spirits in cut crystal. Aaaaahhh ... I sank into a lush maroon cocoon, and it was a heady habit-forming moment. "Where to, Mr. Faith?" the anonymous voice with the cap on asked. "Whisky A-Go-Go, mate." Oh please let this very moment last for fucking ever. It was all slo-mo; Davy reaching for the button that closes the partition, Davy pouring himself a hit of Scotch out of the elegant shimmering bottle, Davy turning to me with that devil/angel grin I had seen on the cover of a hundred magazines. "You're a real looker, darlin'," he said. "It's fuckin' great you had the balls to make a dash for it." I told him I didn't know what came over me, but I was glad it did, and he drank the whole tumbler full of Scotch in one swallow, pulled me onto his lap, and taking my face in his hands, squeezed my jaw, forcing my mouth open wide. All I could do was open up to receive his kisses, and as soon as I was on the brink of a damp and blissful faint, he dribbled some of the scorching Scotch from his mouth onto my tongue, and bit it hard. I started to throb. "Where's the light around here?" Davy smiled in the dark. "I want to show you something, darlin'." He fiddled around with the knobs and dim light suffused us in a steamy glow. "Look here,"

Davy glanced down and I followed his gaze to where his long pale hands were smoothing the fabric tight across the big bulge in his pants. "Look what you've done to me, you bad, bad girl." I had done the deed with Chico enough times to know what came after the dick got big and hard. I was going to fuck my favourite singer. Here I was in the limousine with my hero, and I was going to have his very own penis INSIDE me. It really was almost too much to bear. He seemed content just to kiss me during that long rainy ride from Long Beach to the Whisky A-Go-Go, over and over and over again, even though I would have done anything he might have conjured up. I was struggling to keep my mitts off his bulge—which stayed hard the entire forty-five minutes—because I was hoping he would realize I was a respectable girl. Besides Chico, the only other person I had slept with was a sweet guy named Jimmy, who was the road manager for the Byrds. He had a major crush on me, and I learned the exquisite art of giving head in his one-room bachelor pad on Sweetzer Avenue. I still consider it an art, and I am a Master Artiste. I deserve some special award. It all has

How far can you get it down your throat without gagging?

to do with intensely craving that cock, and besides, a little power over the male member never did a girl any harm. How far can you get it down your throat without gagging? That's the BIG question. Gagging is not conducive to a romantic moment. Ha ha. It really does depend on how big it is. Sometimes I feel sorry for a guy with a giant one because he can only get it halfway down your throat before … Oops, back to the story.

As I was pondering Davy Faith's bulge in the limo, we pulled up in front of the Whisky and he pulled two little blue tablets out of his modified jacket pocket and said, "Take one, Blush." Take one, Blush. Hmmmm. I had avoided LSD because I saw what it did to a few of my friends. They made utter assholes out of themselves and didn't seem to mind. The universe apparently loomed into the room, the whites of their eyes turned crimson and they ground their molars together in a sublime plea for release. It looked like a whole lot of fun that I wasn't interested in having. But the impact of Davy saying my name, and smiling at me like THAT, prompted me to take one of the tablets from his outstretched palm. When it came down to swallowing it, I stalled. "What is it?" I wondered sweetly. "Extremely good mescaline," he said, putting a tablet under his tongue. "I don't argue with Bob Dylan, my darlin', and you know what he said." I racked my brain to come up with the correct Bob Dylan lyric. The possibilities, as they say, were endless. "You know something's happening, but you don't know what it is, do you, Blush Justice?" I asked hopefully. He tossed back his raven curls and laughed, almost maniacally. "Mr. Dylan spoke eloquently to me when he said, 'You shouldn't let other people get your kicks for you.'" He paused dramatically, downing the remainder of the Jack Daniels, "And I don't, Blush, (dot dot dot) neither should you." All these years later I realize I was being heartily connived and manipulated by his fame, glory and that enchanting, noble, romantic accent like King fucking Arthur. Needless to say I swallowed it whole, including the mescaline. Before we climbed out of the womb and into the neon light, he kissed me wetly and said, "I hope you don't have anything important to do tomorrow," and my favourite line by my favourite heroine in my favourite novel slipped out of my Yardley slickered lips, "It's O.K. Davy, (dot dot dot) Tomorrow is Another Day."

The crowd of multicoloured teen-dreams that moved groovily around the Whisky stopped for a few seconds of stunned silence as they realized Davy Faith was in their midst. It was kind of eerie, that quiet breath-held moment. Suspended animation. One girl snapped out of it, yelping with delight, and headed for us when Davy flashed me past the big, black body-guard and into one of those red Naugahyde booths in the back. The centre booth, mind you. The only way to fly.

Big Brother and the Holding Company were in the middle of their set, and everybody was in a frenzied, frantic condition. They went mad when Janis got down on the floor and pleaded with each and every one of them to take it take it take it, and I'm clutching the slim bicep of Davy Faith, seeing little golden twinkles appear right in the middle of thin air! Wow! Far out! Wait a minute! I can see right INTO those little twinkles, right down to where colour is BORN!! Wait wait wait!!! Maybe right UP to where colour is born! Far far far fuck-ing out! It dawned on me that Davy was moving his hand slowly up and down my arm, up and down, up and down. It felt like he had hot oil on his fingertips. I turned to him and saw that he was sparkling at me, those very same golden twinkles pouncing into me from his pitch-blue eyes. He had willed me to look at him. Who the fuck was I to resist? Just as Davy bent to eat my face, Sebastian and Ian slid into the booth with two glamorous garish girls I recognized as the GTO's, a very strange all-girl Frank Zappa group that hung out with famous English boys. One of them was wearing a lot of pink feather boas, and the scary one had coins hanging out of her ears and ringed eyes like a gypsy racoon. Sebastian smiled at me like an angel descending and kissed my hand. I could feel Davy's searing gaze like scalding pin-pricks as he pulled my hand away from Sebastian's lips. Very very dramatic. Sebastian just kept smiling beatifically as all the twinkles were gobbled up into his porcelain skin where I'm sure they remained while Davy and I fled up the back steps and into the tiny backstage bath-room. "I want to be alone with you," he moaned, pushing me against the graffiti'd wall, slip-ping his hand up my dress and into my panties. He touched me softly, stroking me to the beat of so-and-so's drums, sliding his long fingers in and out, in and out, whispering sleazy nonsense in my ear until I was a slippery liquid substance on the concrete floor. Holding his creamy fingers in front of my face, he put them in his mouth and licked them. "Mmmmm-mmm, baby, you taste like a sweet little virgin. I'll bet you haven't had many, have you?" I shook my head no, and that action sent me swirling in a whirlwind of spinning graffiti, and then I was back in the limo, riding the elevator at the Hyatt House, sitting on Davy's bed while he pulled the ripped gauzy dress up over my head. I can remember the moment he released his cock from bondage like it was ten minutes ago; a big, proud hunk of meat sway-ing in front of my awed eyes, and I was so damn high that nothing else existed except

That's the BIG question.

my mouth and his member. I became one with that big rod and when he came, a geyser of salty-sweet molten lava shot down my throat and I felt honoured and privileged to take it, take it, take it. I was too far gone to notice if Davy was as high as I was, besides, his face was buried in my pussy and as he sucked intently on my clit, shock waves reverberated up my spine one after the other until the screams escaping from me prompted some jealous goon in the next room to pound on the wall, briefly busting up my moment of bliss. But by this time the emotional input, steamy sex and extremely good mescaline had bombarded my bursting brain, rendering it incapable of further stimuli. I passed out hot.

II

The sun poked through the awful ochre-flowered drapes, grinding my sodden sleep to a mortified halt. I was alone. What happened? Where was Davy? I raised up in the rumpled bed and saw myself in a gilt-edged mirror on the opposite wall. I was a fright for sore eyes. The wreckage of my Maybelline clung to my cheeks, my chin was a mass of shiny red razor burn and my hair resembled a wanton stack of hay. Maybe I had looked better in the glory of sleep, please God. Davy must have woken up next to me and thought he was having a bad dream, but wait! Hadn't it been glorious? Didn't fireworks go off all over the world? I prodded my muggy mind, going through all the mental motions of the previous evening's fore-play. Hmmm … Aaaaahhhh, yes, mmmmmm … Oh my God, I had not gotten fucked! I had konked out on a rock and roll great before penetration could take place! My humiliation was abject, it surrounded me like dead air. Where was Davy? Maybe he had gone to Cleveland or some other far-off lame-brained town. Maybe he was in the bathroom. "Davy?" My voice came out an abrasive squeak. The piped-in air hummed all by itself, the infant refrigerator churned. Maybe he left me a note? I struggled out of the sheets and trotted all around the room seeking a piece of evidence that would prove Davy had been there. Remnants of room service that anyone could have eaten sat there on a trolley turning rancid. A couple of wine bottles full of cigarette butts stood mute on the ugly table next to the bed where scraps of paper full of hopeful phone numbers sat in a discarded heap. Mama said there'd be days like this, there'd be days like this, my mama said. Speaking of my mama, I wondered if she noticed I hadn't come home. Maybe she wasn't even up yet. What time was it? I dialled the operator only to find out it was almost noon. Why hadn't Davy left me a note? I started to slide down into that self-pity pit when the phone jingle-jangled like Jim McGuinn's guitar (he had yet to weird out and change his name to Roger-Wilco-Over-and-Out), sending me into an instant spasm. Should I answer it? What if it's some girlfriend in England? Fuck it. "Will you be checking out this morning?" a cheery voice inquired of me. "Yes, ma'am," I managed to

> *I yanked them up and started to cry at the same moment. Sobsobsob*

croak and wearily began to gather up my clothes. Luckily, my pink panties were around my ankle; I yanked them up and started to cry at the same moment. Sobsobsob. Used and abused by a major rock star. I supposed it was better than being abused by the guy who cleaned my parents' carpets.

Perfect teen anguish ensued, exquisite in its entirety. OhGodJesusMotherMary. I can still feel it. The pain was piercing, I was a shattered husk.

Do you believe in (magic) love at first sight? Actually, love overnight? Being IN love, I suppose, is like being IN the pool. Or IN the ocean. Immersed, dripping and sopping from it, leaving tell-tale footprints all over the place when you get out. Could I function well enough to get myself home? Then what? I was stared at by visiting businessmen as I stood barefoot and bedraggled in the corner of the elevator, holding my garter belt and high-heeled sandals. They thought I was a hippie harlot. Fuck 'em. They would probably beat their meat with me in mind for the next several days. Ha ha ha.

No one was around when I got home, after hitchhiking through Laurel Canyon on the back of a numbingly loud motorcycle, and in a slow-moving Pontiac complete with bob-bing-head Jesus and sincere, concerned soul. It was a dismal Sunday afternoon, and all the doors were closed. What else was new? I got in bed and stared at Davy's face grinning down at me from all four walls. I had almost made love with my hero. Oh well, I had been inti-mate with my idol and nobody could take that away from me. I called Tina and started from the beginning, and she held my hand over the phone, even though she was so jealous I could just see her eyes getting narrow and slitty.

I told my mom that I had spent the night with Tina, and I had rotten cramps, woe is me, I'm going to stay in bed. She was concerned and made me a cup of hot chocolate. I felt guilty for fibbing in her face. I wished I could have told her how Davy's fingers felt when I was flat against the bathroom wall at the Whisky, spread-eagled like I was being sexually frisked. She wouldn't have been amused. It must have been a hard time to be a mom. I mean, she had to have known that I was doing some questionable things. She preferred to pretend I wasn't. The riots and love-ins were on TV and she looked down at her crossword puzzle, hoping to avoid my face on the screen. I caught sight of myself for a split second on the seven o'clock news. I had on false Twiggy eyelashes and daisies painted on my face. History in the making.

AUTHENTIC CORRESPONDENCE SENT TO SYLVIE "MELODY" RANCOURT

From the Bottom...

MAY 1987

First letter

HELLO MELODY!

I AM SENDING THIS LETTER IN CARE OF THE TELEVISION STATION, SO I HOPE IT WILL REACH YOU.

CAMÉRA 87

I LOVED THAT FEATURE ON YOU, MELODY. YOU'RE AN AMAZING WOMAN-- CREATIVE, ENTHUSIASTIC, FULL OF HIDDEN RESOURCES.

MY NAME IS DANIELLE, I'M 23 AND COME FROM TOULOUSE IN SOUTHWESTERN FRANCE. I AM GENTLE, SENSUAL AND FEMININE.

I TOO HAVE WORKED MANY YEARS AS A NUDE DANCER (IN FRANCE) BUT SINCE ARRIVING IN QUEBEC CITY, I JUST SERVE IN A RESTAURANT.

I FOUND YOU INSTANTLY LIKEABLE ON T.V. AND DECIDED TO WRITE. IT WOULD PLEASE ME NO END IF YOU COULD SEND ME TWO PICTURES OF YOURSELF ALONG WITH A FEW WORDS.

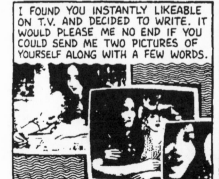

IN JULY I AM MOVING IN WITH MY *COUSINE* IN MONTREAL. PERHAPS AFTER EXCHANGING A FEW LETTERS, WE COULD MEET AND GET TO KNOW EACH OTHER?

TRANSLATED & VISUALIZED by JACQUES BOIVIN

THEN, WITHOUT UTTERING A WORD, SHE SUDDENLY PULLED ME OVER HER KNEES—

LIFTED MY SCHOOLGIRL'S SKIRT—

PULLED DOWN MY PANTIES—

AND GAVE ME AT LEAST 30 VIGOROUS SLAPS ON MY NAKED BUTTOCKS.

(SPANKING IS QUITE COMMON AND POPULAR IN FRANCE, YOU KNOW!)

THIS EXPERIENCE PROFOUNDLY TROUBLED ME AS IT BROUGHT FORTH ALL KINDS OF NEW & UNEXPECTED SEXUAL SENSATIONS.

EVER SINCE THAT POWERFUL SPANKING, MELODY, I DREAM THAT A YOUNG WOMAN WOULD AGREE TO TREAT ME WITH TENDER SEVERITY...

SHE WOULD SPANK ME AFFECTIONATELY AS I LAY ON MY STOMACH...

...THEN KISS AND CARESS MY FLUSTERED CHEEKS...

...AS WELL AS MY VAGINA, NOW WET WITH DESIRE!

I OFTEN DREAM OF THIS, MELODY!

I HOPE I'M NOT OFFENDING YOU WITH MY SECRET LONGING.

EVEN THOUGH I'VE BEEN A NUDE DANCER, I AM NEVERTHELESS A CHASTE AND MODEST GIRL.

PRETTY PLEASE, SEND ME ONE OR TWO PHOTOGRAPHS OF YOURSELF... SENSUAL & EROTIC!

Miriam Jones

Fingerprints

S HE HOLDS A CRISP NEW FIVE-DOLLAR BILL IN HER HAND. SHE RUNS IT THROUGH her fingers as she waits in line.

(Imagine you are in a little room with dry wooden floors, a high ceiling and cracked paint. Imagine you have one, tall window with thin, blowing curtains. Imagine that it is early summer and the noises of the city shimmer up from below. You sit on your kitchen chair and look out the window. Directly opposite and a little above you there is an enormous billboard. On the billboard, a woman lies on her stomach wearing men's briefs and undershirt. She looks over her shoulder at you and smiles. A small mole rides on the fluted curve of her lip. Her buttocks lift slightly into the air; there is just enough space between her hips and the floor for a hand to slip in. Her legs are unnaturally long. You cannot look out the window without seeing at least part of her. Sometimes you use the billboard for a meditation aid.)

She always buys her magazine from the newsstand; a subscription might mean wrinkled pages, and besides, she would have to wait for delivery. She usually buys it on the first day it hits the stores; she begins to check the magazine racks around the second week of each month. She always reaches back into the fresh pile and pulls out an untouched copy with no fingerprints or creases disturbing the shiny cover. After she has read it, it will remain in the basket beside the bathroom sink, water-spotted pages thick with talcum powder and hairs fallen from her brush. But not yet. She will flip through, over and over, when she sits on the toilet.

(Some models are so light you could pick them up and carry them away. Some are so thin you want to take them to a restaurant and buy them a good meal and watch them eat. You want to cry when you see their little hunched shoulders. Surely they would break if they were touched. You try to picture them having sex, but you cannot. You feel like a sadist for even imagining it.)

She has bought *Vogue* since she was a teenager. Then she was at a friend's apartment once, where she saw *Elle* and *Mirabella* in a rack beside the bath. She stayed in there for twenty minutes, leafing through, and that month she began to buy them as well. The friend discusses whether the beauty tips were helpful. She cannot remember, herself. Another friend used to buy *Marie-Claire*, saying it was to help her to learn French. She did not know if she liked *Marie-Claire*, it was disconcerting, not understanding the text beneath the photographs. And the models were different: young, and European. Photographed outdoors, with overlong wisps of hair and particles of sand blowing into their squinting eyes beneath their hats. Schoolgirls on holidays. She felt a vague sense of guilt looking at them.

(Some models have coltish legs; you could tip them over and take them to the ground and lie there, entangled in hose and platform heels.)

Some times when she looks at photographs, she thinks of the models, alone, exposed to the eyes of the photographers and lighting men. What were those men thinking? When they saw the fabric slide across a nipple, away from a breast, did they want to slip their hands in? When the make-up man had to touch up her back, her chest, did he take longer than he needed to? When she lay there in the sand, eyes half-closed, did they want to lower themselves on top of her? Did they?

Of course, she thinks, women work on photo shoots too, and most of the men are gay, and it is just a job to all of them, and she is conjuring a scenario from a straight man's porno movie rather than a real fashion shoot. But. But. She looks back at the page. The model lies on the silver sand at night. The shadow of a breast, overcome by gravity, can be seen between her arm and the fabric of her evening gown. Her head is thrown back; she offhandedly offers her throat with the air of one who no longer even notices. In green chiffon.

(All models' skin, despite variations in shade, has the same matte texture. They have no pores on their faces. You could not lick their cheeks because you would ruin the effect, but you could stroke them, softly. They have no hair on their bodies. You can see no pubic hair, no matter which way you turn the page. They have no nicks or bumps or chicken skin; they would feel the same to your hand, all over. You cannot think of your body at the same time; there is a wall. You inhabit a different universe.)

(Myth #1: It's all in the lighting and make-up; underneath, they're normal women like you and me.)

(Myth #2: There are normal women.)

There is a photo-spread of Jamaica. There are shots of an African-American model wearing resort clothes, standing with a fisherman on a wharf. With children in a street. With a middle-aged woman in a market. The model looks strange beside these people: a bug-eyed creature, all elbows and iridescence. She flips through until she comes to a shot of the model alone on the beach, the tide rushing up her thighs; and at night in a pavilion, the wind lifting her skirt, startled. She looks at that page.

(Sometimes, even though you are a straight woman, you want to gently knead a model's soft breasts and hold them in your hand. What is your favourite type of breast? Do you like them firm and compact, pale white skin with blue veins showing, rosy nipple? Do you prefer the ski-slope shape, uptilted and heavy underneath? Do those breasts make your palms itch to take their weight? Do you like full, round breasts, like melons, or do you prefer next-to-no breasts on a muscular torso? Do full, warm, round breasts that you could gently squash in your hands above a sparrow-thin ribcage and tiny waist make you weep? Do you want to be like that? Touch that? Be touched like that? What are your breasts like?)

She has just bought the September issue. It is the thickest of the year. It has a satisfying heft in her hand. The pages are crisp and shiny, and the smell of perfume stings her eyes. It is a promise in her desk drawer, all day. That night, her mother telephones while she is reading; as she answers her questions, she gently brushes the tips of her fingers across the pages. She is impatient.

(Myth #3: You wouldn't even recognize them if you saw them on the bus.)

She has a favourite model who looks like a space alien: all huge eyes, gamine hair and pursed lips. Oversized hands, knees and feet. This model has a smile to stop your heart, and looking at her photograph, deep down she knows that this woman is oblivious to her success.

(What would you say to a woman like that, if you met her? Would you want to touch her? Talk to her? Eat her? Pretend she wasn't there? Be her friend?)

She is lying on her bed. The magazine is between her legs, tangled in the sheets. She presses her thighs together; she thinks of nighttime, beaches, no, a pool, hot sun, tied spread-eagled to a lawn chair while a man bends over her and does things with his hands. Overcome and dazzled by the sun. A butler brings out a tray of drinks but is too professional to stare. He is used to it. The man slides down her bathing-suit straps and exposes her breasts. He rubs an ice cube on her nipples. She moans and twists. He lightly slaps her breasts. It is her on the lounge; it is not her. It is her, looking. Looking at her. At herself.

She does not think she would like anyone to slap her. Not her fleshy breasts.

(Do you have fantasies about suddenly having a different body? You were in a horrible traffic accident and after a series of painful operations, you are unrecognizable. Scientists perfect the technique to transfer the mind to a different body. Aliens take you and clone you. Then, you are ... you are ...

You are in the magazine. You will be on the beach at night forever, and the butler will bring the tray as you are lying by the pool. Your hair will always be blowing out behind you, and there will always be hands on you. On your firm, round breasts. Sliding down your back and cupping your buttocks. Running up your calves, your legs. Fingers slipping under the edge of the elastic where your thigh meets your hip. Fingers slipping in, always.)

She licks the shiny pictures, slowly at first, and then with increasing frenzy. Spit dribbles off her chin and into the cleft between the pages. The paper becomes so moist that it rips; she take it into her mouth with her lips, like a horse with a sugar cube. She eats the magazine, slowly, in a trance. Afterwards, she sits by the window, a halo of ink around her mouth and a distended belly. The few remaining pages drop from her blackened fingers, fall and fan out over the floor. She idly wonders, staring into the middle distance, how many calories there are in paper.

Carol Lazare
Addicted to Love

Ida Roseant (pronounced Rose-ant) is fortyish and celibate, has been for five years. At her annual physical/internal examination with Dr. Bernice Leitner, good family friend and physician to Ida's deceased mother, Molly, Dr. Leitner encourages Ida to "get creative" in order to meet somebody. She believes that Ida "should be having sex" because "humans need to touch other humans, skin to skin, dear."

Randy Neville, Ida's boss, throws another "should" onto her "would" pile.

INTERIOR. L'AMOUR BUILDING. RANDY NEVILLE'S OFFICE. DOWNTOWN TORONTO. DAY.

Randy is the second-generation owner of L'Amour Publishing. He's late forties with no sex appeal but a definite twinkle in his eye and a dour sense of humour. Ida has been working for L'Amour for ten years as one of their most productive writers of romance novels. She started out as a proofreader and worked her way up. Her pen names are Iris Queensley and Isabelle Pendent.

Ida enters Randy's office.

IDA
How are you today Randy?

RANDY
One day nearer the grave.

Ida giggles as she has for years at this response.

RANDY
Meadowland Kisses sold out. We're going into a second printing. Congratulations Iris.

IDA
Isabelle.

RANDY
Isabelle Pendent? She's back is she?

IDA
Her leave of absence is over. Time for Iris Queensley to take maternity leave or something.

RANDY
Or perhaps pressing family matters demand Ms. Queensley's attention in South Africa.

IDA
[*giggling*] Pressing indeed. So? What's the verdict Randy?

RANDY
None yet. We're still debating.

IDA
About what? Aren't you going to go ahead with the erotica book?

RANDY
On the contrary. We're convinced that's the only avenue to take with the growing numbers of celibate readers. We're debating about you Ida. You're our best writer and the obvious one to take on this new venture. However, your first draft leaves a lot to be desired. If it was romance we were selling it would be perfect. But erotica is what we want and I'm afraid erotica is not what we got.

IDA
For instance?

He takes out her manuscript and reads.

RANDY
On page 23. "Flannery watched him in silhouette through his candle-lit tent. With each layer of buckskin that fell from Gregor's exquisitely moulded physique, Flannery's pulse quickened with anticipation. So close and yet so far away she saw his manhood bulging in the shadows."

Randy, non-plussed, looks at Ida, expecting a response.

IDA
What's the problem?

RANDY
It's not erotic. It doesn't take the leap. What's happening inside Flannery while she's watching this man? What is she fantasizing about? What would she like him to do with his "manhood"? And, more importantly, what would she like to do with "it"?

Pause.

IDA
I don't know.

RANDY
We have to feel some heat.

IDA
Let me work on it.

RANDY
You've got one month Ida. That's all I can give you.

Ida meets with Luba, her younger sister by two years, at their fitness club for a StairMaster workout and a little whirlpool and sauna.

Luba is impatient with Ida generally, but particularly with the euphemisms required in romance writing. She believes, "You can do better than 'manhood.' How about tool or bald-headed mouse?" To Ida's concern that "I haven't seen a real one in years, let alone know what I would want to do with it," Luba advises her to go to California Movies, a porn shop that she frequents, or Fantasies. "You get to see real live penises there."

Ida, out of curiosity, checks out the photos of the male strippers at the entrance to Fantasies and ends up at California Movies deliberating whether or not she should go in. Mrs. Resten, Ida's sister Merle's next-door neighbour, shows up and gives her a tour.

MRS. RESTEN

These here are yer straight flicks. Yer mainstream, Hollywood stuff with porn stars and stories, y'know like regular pictures except they don't pretend they're doin' it. They're really doin' it and you get to see it and they do it with a lot of different people for most of the movie.

Much to the disgust of Merle, Ida's older sister by two years, Luba and Ida spend an evening watching the porn movie Ida picked out with Mrs. Resten's advice. Ida is amazed by the technique of the stars, the "skill" as Luba calls it, referring to the "sword swallowing trick" which Ida attempts to simulate with a Coke bottle. Impressed as she is with the open-gullet technique, the practice of "spraying" leaves her cold and she insists that she wants "something to stimulate me not obliterate me".

Luba takes her to Fantasies, a male strip-club that vibrates with the laughter, screams and high spirits of a crowd of women. Jules the Jive Man comes on stage in dark glasses, a white T-shirt and black pants, carrying a saxophone. The cool jazz of John Coltrane is heard over the sound system as Jules lip-synchs with his sax. Ida is agog. He puts his sax down and then struts his stuff. He strips completely and parades in front of Ida. She screams at the top of her voice.

In the next couple of days Ida attempts to impart the impact of these vicarious sexual adventures to her writing. To no avail.

Merle's fifteen-year-old daughter, Morgan, runs away. Ida is Morgan's confidante and knows where to find her. That night she rides her bike out to the breakwater and she and Morgan ride home together.

EXTERIOR. DOWNTOWN STREET. NIGHT.
Ida is riding down a street heading home, after dropping off Morgan, then makes an abrupt turn around and heads full speed in the opposite direction.

INTERIOR. FANTASIES.
Jules is into his number and starting to strip.

EXTERIOR. FANTASIES.
Ida hurriedly dismounts her bike and locks it to a parking meter. She dashes for the door.

INTERIOR. FANTASIES.
Jules is working on his G-string.

INTERIOR. FANTASIES. STAIRWELL.
Ida, two stairs at a time, runs up.

INTERIOR. FANTASIES.
Ida at the entrance to the club watches Jules remove his G-string and start his strut down the runway to sounds of John Coltrane. She is a goner.

INTERIOR. FANTASIES. VARIOUS NIGHTS.
Sequence of scenes: Ida alone, on different nights. Ida observes a woman standing at the end of the runway with a five-dollar bill in her cleavage. Fireman Jack leans over and plucks it out with his lips.

Ida observes another woman at the end of the runway with a five-dollar bill tucked into the top of her slacks. Beau the Butler crouches down and removes it between his teeth.

Ida observes how the private, one-on-one performances are set up.

Ida watches Jules sitting with a couple of young women during a break.

Ida catches Jules' eye during one of his performances.

Ida stands by the runway with a five-dollar bill tucked into her cleavage. Jules leans over and plucks it out with his teeth.

Ida watches Jules do a private, one-on-one performance for her.

INTERIOR. IDA'S APARTMENT. NIGHT.
Ida is trying to work at her computer. She is distracted and drifts off into fantasy imagining herself with Jules.

... They are at the club during one of the dance breaks. He asks her to dance and she does. She is fully clothed; he is naked. As close as they can be without touching, his eyes reach for her as though they are hands ...

The computer starts to buzz and breaks her fantasy. She finds the keyboard stuck between her legs. Her pulse is racing.

IDA'S BATHROOM.
Ida splashes water on her face. She observes herself in the mirror and sees a very determined look.

IDA'S BEDROOM.
Ida slips one of her mid-calf-length dresses over her head. She rummages in the bottom drawer of her dresser and finds, way at the back, an old crumpled box of condoms. She takes one out and puts it into her wallet.

INTERIOR. FANTASIES. NIGHT.
Ida sits alone at a table in the centre of the room, a determined look etched on her face. She is like an island of controlled calm in the middle of a stormy sea. The usual screaming and waving

is going on as Jules performs his number. She does not react to any of his moves and when he struts down the runway and flashes his fabulous smile and every other fabulous thing at her, she, uncharacteristically, shows no reaction, only a deeply determined stare.

IDA'S P.O.V.
Jules leaves the stage.

Hip-hop music is blaring and the MC announces a short break and invites customers to dance. Women rush onto the stage.

Jules begins to cross the room in Ida's direction. He stops momentarily at the bar to pick up a Coke. He looks at Ida, looks at the stage, then walks toward her. He is in front of her, three feet away.

JULES
Wanna sip?

He extends his Coke to her.

WIDE SHOT TO INCLUDE IDA.
Ida takes the bottle and tilts it back and takes a good long swig. She attempts the open-gullet technique and ends up sputtering. Jules pats her a couple of times on the back and she recovers. He removes his hand, slowly, from her back.

JULES
Not having fun tonight?

IDA
I'm preoccupied.

JULES
Other things on your mind.

IDA
Uh-huh.

JULES
I think I know what.

Pause.

IDA
[*fixes her determined look right smack at him*]
I think you do.

JULES
[*puts his hand into his pocket and pulls out a card and hands it to her*]
Call me. Any time.

Jules walks away. Ida reads the card. "Jules Ventures Inc. Exclusive Clientele, $200.00 an hour. Visa, AMEX, Mastercard accepted."

INTERIOR. FITNESS CLUB. DAY.
Ida and Luba are on the StairMasters.

IDA
It's actually come to this. I'm actually considering paying for it!

LUBA
It's a good thing he takes Visa.

IDA
I still have to pay for it!

LUBA
But not in one shot.

IDA
You think it's O.K. to pay for sex.

LUBA
The best way to get it.

IDA
When did you become so jaded?

LUBA
I'm not. I'm really happy. I have very clear expectations of men. I want nothing more than sex from them. What better way to get it than from a professional.

IDA
It seems very straightforward.

LUBA
He turns you on and he wouldn't have given you his card if he wasn't attracted.

IDA
You think so? My God.

LUBA
The card says exclusive clientele, right?

IDA
Uh-huh.

LUBA
You will have the best sex of your entire life.

IDA
In an hour?

LUBA
For God's sake I.! It's on your Visa!

IDA
How long!? Two hours?!

LUBA
Two or three.

IDA
That's six hundred dollars! That's an emergency root canal!

LUBA
It's one unforgettable night after five forgettable years of celibacy. How can you worry about the money?

IDA
What am I going to say?

LUBA
It's not like making a cold call. You already know him and he knows exactly why you're calling. You don't have to have a conversation. Tell him the date, the time and your address and hang up.

INTERIOR. IDA'S APARTMENT. VARIOUS ROOMS. NIGHT.
Ida is tidying up. She's dressed casually in one of her mid-calf-length dresses. There is a buzz. She answers the phone.

IDA
Hi. 333.

She is excruciatingly nervous. She rushes to the bathroom and splashes water on her face. There is a knock at the door. She rushes to the front door and opens it. Jules is there and fully clothed. He looks good in clothes too.

IDA
Come in. Come in. Would you like some wine? Sparkling water?

JULES
Water would be good.

Ida leaves for a moment and returns with two bottles and glasses with ice and a bowl of fruit. She sits with him on the couch. He selects a peach and with his Swiss Army knife cuts it into four perfect wedges.

JULES
Peeled?

IDA
No, that's okay. Is that the Explorer?

JULES
Explorer II.

IDA
I've got the Golfer. Not that I golf. But it has this cute little toothpick in it. I think they're amazing.

Jules focuses on Ida, taking her in, without distraction, with complete concentration, her eyes, her chin, her hair, her shoulders, her hands. He's very good at his job.

JULES
Yeah. They are amazing.

Pause.

JULES
I wanted to thank you for the advance payment. That way we don't have to worry about money all night.

IDA
But I only paid for two hours.

JULES
Yeah. I didn't mean I was going to be here all night.

IDA
Oh right. You just used that expression, all night but it doesn't mean all night.

JULES
Yeah. I don't charge the same rate for all night anyway.

IDA
Oh you don't.

JULES
Yeah. It's kind of a package thing for special clients.

IDA
Regulars?

JULES
Yeah. Kinda.

IDA
How's your water?

JULES
Good. How's yours?

IDA
Fine.

JULES
Great apartment.

IDA
Thank you.

JULES
You're a great-looking woman, Ida. I noticed you the first time you came into the club. You didn't look like a receptionist.

IDA
I worked as a receptionist one summer while I was in school, for a lawyer.

JULES
You looked kind of mysterious to me. In the long dress you had on. It hid you but just made me more curious. Kind of like this long thing you have on now. Makes me curious about what's underneath.

IDA
Just little ole me.
[*she brushes her hand through her hair*]

JULES
Did you know that when you lift your hand like that and brush it through your hair, your dress moves all over your body.

IDA
You mean like this.

She brushes her hand through her hair again. With his hand in the air, an inch away from her body, he traces the movement of the dress over the shoulder, her chest, a breast, a hip, a thigh and a leg.

JULES
I wanna move all over you just like your dress.

IDA
O.K.

They stand and bring their clothed bodies within an inch of each other, nose to nose, eye to eye. Ida raises her hand and brushes it through her hair and Jules, no hands, rubs his gorgeous frame up and down, back and forth over her entire body. She stretches her arms as far as she can above her head. Facing her he raises his arms and clasps her hands in his, then with his hands and lips traces every inch of her.

IDA
I can just imagine what will happen if we take our clothes off.

And with that he pulls his T-shirt over his head, he undoes his silk pants and they fall to the floor. Ida sees a body very familiar to her. Now, however, she's allowed to touch. She walks around behind him.

IDA
Don't look.

She pulls her dress up over her head and approaches him from behind. She puts her arms around his beautifully moulded shoulders and lifts one leg around his thigh. Jules closes his eyes for a lingering moment. He smooths his hand over her thigh.

IDA'S BEDROOM.
Ida and Jules together in a close shot from the shoulders up. They are sweating and barely able to speak.

IDA
Jules! I have to stop!

JULES
You've never passed this point, have you?

IDA
I'm going to shatter into a million pieces!

JULES
You're almost there.

IDA
 I'm there already! I'm there!

JULES
Somewhere else.

She's stunned and looks at him quizzically.

JULES
Ecstasy.

She grabs his gorgeous head of hair with both hands and pulls him to her. She emits a low animal growl from way, way down in her primordial soul.

Jules is the "stimulation" Ida needs to get her creative juices flowing and she completes a second draft of Buckskin and Lace. *Ida, however, doesn't have as clear a line on sex, men and love as Luba does. More like Merle, the lines for her are blurry and she falls for Jules and he reciprocates. The fallout from this odd coupling strains the bonds between Ida and her sisters.*

There is nothing quite as painful to the soul as the judgement of family, and the sisters lay out a feast of it for each other. They do realize, however, after suffering the discomforts of bloating and gorging, that there's no right way to fall in love.

I don't know why.

It's just that sometimes I get bored.

And then I do these things.

And then one night …

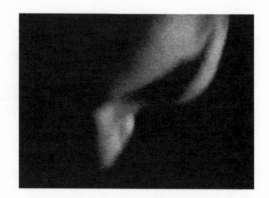

… I saw this girl.

I didn't know what to do next.
And so …

I became obsessed.

Will you dine with me tonight?

A woman I know.

And I thought
happiness had passed me by.

Gigi the Galaxy Girl

For the Love of a Good Toaster

J UNE SQUEEZED A FISH-PASTE TUBE BETWEEN HER PALM AND THE EDGE OF HER
plastic plate and smeared the grey remains onto a stale biscuit. She popped it into her
mouth and allowed the cracker to dissolve slowly. Bored with her reconstituted dinner,
she mounded a blob of mashed potatoes and squashed it through the fork tines. She leaned
back in her chair and reached for the vid control box, licked her index finger and tapped the
channel box. Nibbling another dry biscuit, June smiled and selected a now familiar infomer-
cial in progress.

"Now, we will toast one slice of white bread at a time, then, several slices, and finally con-
secutive batches in quick succession." The camera panned over the counter to take in the
loaves of sandwich bread; french, raisin, and rye-cut loaves; bagels and english muffins.

"Here we have our four-slice luncheonette-style model. Note that this well-designed
machine has separate controls for each pair of slots. Our versatile model features dual controls for simultaneous slices of light or dark toast. The Toast Shade colour selector brings
perfect results every time."

June picked at her potatoes with a plastic fork and stared as the announcer loaded his
toaster and fingered the electronic controls. "Until EARTH-HOME's patented improve-
ments, the manufacture of the pop-up toaster had changed little since Toastmaster intro-
duced the device in 1926. As you know, electrical wires raise the bread's surface temperature
to more than 300 degrees Fahrenheit, which causes the natural sugars and starches to caramelize.
Add too much heat and the sugars and grain fibres will turn to carbon and the toast will
become inedible. This is a delicate scientific operation. At EARTH-HOME, performance
is paramount."

The studio audience hushed as the announcer became serious. He crossed his arms and
stepped from behind the counter to face the studio audience. "Friends, we at EARTH-
HOME understand the needs of you, the off-world colonist. We respect our customers and

produce only highly efficient, lightweight, reliable machines." Pausing in his address, the announcer smiled, turned his back to the screen with a flourish and caught the springing toast with one hand. "We deliver everything you could possibly want from your household appliances, and more."

The camera scanned over the faces of the neatly dressed and freshly scrubbed audience members as they nodded in rapt agreement. June nodded, too, at the vid screen, her mouth full of fish-paste and crumbs, as the camera moved in for a close-up of four golden slices fanned over a blood-red plate. "YOU want … no, you demand … that your toaster produce evenly browned toast, over and over and over again."

June sighed as a buzz at the apartment-unit intercom interrupted her vid program. Setting her plate on top of the vid box, June scrambled to her feet. In two strides she was at the door, rubbing her hands over her coverall trousers to rid them of fish-paste. She touched the control-panel release, and the door swung wide. A uniformed Mars-Postal employee stood just outside, holding an oversized package. "So soon," June mumbled stupidly, her eyes widening. The postal employee blinked back at her from behind regulation safety goggles and mouth filter and glanced perfunctorily at the identi-card June wrestled from her coverall pocket. With a barely audible thank you, June grasped the parcel and stumbled backward into her unit. As the door mechanisms whirred and clicked behind her, June stood for a moment to admire the box decorated with large customs and postage stickers. She brushed away the last pink granules of Martian sand still clinging to the gummed labels. Her fingers traced the words: EARTH-HOME APPLIANCE MANUFACTURERS CO.

The vid was ignored for now. June squatted next to her armchair and placed the large box directly before her. "Now, let's see what we've got here," June said, shyly running her index finger along the edges of the sealed box. Finding a niche, her fingers slipped under a box flap. June held her breath when her fingernails punctured and bit into the plastic sealing tape, cracking a seam like a scar along the box lid. Two lid edges spread open, and June looked inside.

Panic pounded in her chest. The box was filled only with excelsior. Twisting curls of brown wrapping paper. Could they have forgotten …? She relaxed. "No. Not possible." She rocked on her knees and wound a stray paper curl around her fingers. Leaning in closer, June stroked her palm across the surface of the curls and felt the tickle of the rough paper. Her decision made, June raised both hands above the box and plunged them into the mass of twisting curls. Her knuckles grazed the box walls until they collided with an unyielding object. Her hands groped and wrestled it out of the box. She pushed the discarded box aside and untangled the excelsior from chrome and plastic. She drew the object onto her lap and sighed with pleasure. "Ah." It was a beautiful 5-Speed Cyclo-Trol automatic blender.

"The trend toward efficiency need not sacrifice beauty," the vid entoned in a soothing voice, "The sleek lines—the use of chrome instead of plastic, for instance—transform the plain vanilla appliance into an object of domestic delight."

June began her caresses at the top of the blender. She admired the streamlined pitcher as her fingers traced the ridged arrows etched in the glass. Moving downward, her fingers trailed

BLEND

over the Dawn Grey plastic control panel with its five speeds and pulse control. Manufactured for maximum blending satisfaction. Her fingertips brushed over the five Bermuda Pink buttons announcing incremental increases in speed. June savoured their names on her tongue: purée, whip, blend, liquefy and frappé. The turbo-pulse button, an engorged version of the other five, was ignored for the moment. Hands no longer tentative, she stroked the erect rubber buttons, blushing only slightly as her own nipples grew erect in response. Finally, her hands fondled the rounded voluptuousness of the metallic base. There she drew her fingers over the EARTH-HOME insignia embossed on the blender's base like a chrome tattoo. She rubbed the chrome with the heel of her hand, and for a milli-second, her hand left a ghostly print on the cold metal. In a final approving glance, June rose and cradled the blender in the crook of her arm. With her left hand, she wound the trailing cord around her neck like a plucked feather-boa and padded into her tiny kitchenette.

The kitchenette was dominated by a stainless-steel countertop bounded on one end by a water cooler and sink and, on the other, by a microwave. The counter surface was cluttered with several very new kitchen appliances: an electric garlic press, a coffee grinder, a portable cake mixer, a food processor, a juicer. Their electrical cords snaked along the counter

WHIP

and choked the single electrical outlet. June sighed and rested the blender on her left hip. In one movement, she coiled the five appliance cords around her right wrist and yanked them from the outlet. In their place, June inserted the blender cord and rested the appliance with care in the centre of the counter. Lifting the pitcher from its housing, she tipped the rim under the water cooler and allowed several inches of water to fill the pitcher before replacing it. June tested the coolness of the countertop with her open palm and frowned slightly. From under the sink, she drew open a utility drawer and pulled out neatly folded tea towels and insulated oven mitts. She made a neat pyramid in the centre of the counter next to the blender. With the kitchenette prepared, June turned her attention to herself. She turned her hands over and noted that they were sticky with perspiration. Her coveralls seemed heavy and constraining for domestic work. Thoughtfully, June stroked her palms over her stomach. Then, with more decision, she freed her body by sliding a thumb under the Velcro closures of her garment and tearing them open. She shifted her shoulders and allowed her clothes to fall onto the kitchenette floor. Stepping out of the coveralls, dressed only in her cotton muscle shirt and briefs, she was ready.

June drew a kitchen stool up to the lip of the steel counter and climbed up the rungs. She lifted her body onto the shelf and shivered as she felt the shock of the cool steel through her thin cotton underpants. Bare legs swung across the kitchen cabinet drawers until her heels braced her body on the countertop. She swivelled her hips and extended her legs and seated

FRAPPE

herself comfortably on the neat pile of oven mitts and tea towels. June drew her knees up and around the blender, entwining the object with her ankles. She manoeuvred the blender against her damp crotch and clenched her thighs. The blender was anchored and secure.

She tilted her neck and shoulders back and propped herself against the microwave. She allowed her hand to trail along the blender's rubber buttons. Her hand shook slightly as she grasped and flicked the on-switch. She paused and considered a selection from the variable speed control. Their names were etched into her memory: purée, whip, blend, liquefy, and frappé. Her hand lingered over the first selection: PUREE. Her fingertip feathered the rubber button, savouring the moment. Taking a deep breath, June depressed the button firmly and pulled back her hand to fondle her own breast. The blender began to hum, and water swirled quietly inside the pitcher. Hard knotted muscles in her stomach and lower back relaxed under the blender's kneading drone. Restful images of green and orange mashed baby food accompanied sleepy vibrations. Only her desire for a sequential rise in power pulled June from a soothing lethargy. And, of course, curiosity needled her on to further exploration.

June squinted her eyes and glanced at the blender controls. She fondled the second button. Her forefinger grazed and depressed WHIP. Oscillations pulsed through chrome, plastic, cotton and reverberated against her cunt. June contracted and released her leg muscles, imitating the new rhythm of the blender motor. WHIP conjured for June images of stiletto-toed dominatrixes undulating around her bed. Laughing women leaned from above to knead her breasts and comb their long enamelled fingers through her pubic hair. Tassled whips fell in caresses across her inner thighs.

June's fingers moved across the speed-control panel. BLEND and LIQUEFY were thrust sequentially with renewed urgency as June watched liquid swirl higher against the pitcher's glass walls. The pitch of the rotary engine rose an octave, and a whir of energy purred through her dampening bikini. The raw cotton of her underpants itched and confined her. She slipped a finger under the elastic band and lifted her rear until the fabric confined only her thighs. By raising her left leg and tugging the underpants over thigh, knee and ankle, she could slip the cotton briefs off one leg without losing a beat of the blender's pulsations. Her briefs slid down her calf, hovering on her ankle until June kicked her leg free. They fell to the linoleum

LIQUEFY

floor. She recrossed her ankles and manoeuvred her heels against the blender's chrome housing until it could be thrust more deeply onto her labia. Uninhibited vibrations resounded and electrified her body from pelvic bone to clitoris hood.

The final threshold could be resisted no longer. She was insatiable now. Her palm covered the speed controls, and she thumbed the rubber button, FRAPPE. A rise in the appliance's temperature and a surge in power was immediately perceptible. An image of a stalled and burnt-out blender flashed unbidden before June's vision. Her eyes strayed to the power outlet. Still, a power surge was only a remote, though terrifying, possibility. She squeezed her thighs more tightly around the blender as if to ground her electric pleasure. Ripples of energy arced over her body. Panic-induced andrenalin now coursed through her veins and

P U R E E

heightened her visceral response to the sound of the whirring engine, the taste of salt on her lips and the sticky-sweet smell of her throbbing vagina. Her cunt ground to the motor and lubricated the quivering metal. She arched her back and drove her pelvis forward. The throb of the chrome-encased engine sent shivers along her spine, and she rocked with the reverberations. Suddenly, June was spiralling in the blender's whirlpool. A crest washed over her, and she was pulled into the curl. Her breath was ragged and laboured, rising in gasps with each wave of sensation. She was drowning. "Oh, *mon dieu*," she gasped as water splashed and bubbled against the rubber non-slip lid of the glass pitcher.

She exhaled and flicked the blender's off-switch. Residual vibrations dissolved, and the water subsided to an even swirl. June smiled and licked her parched lips. Her knees unclenched and dropped to the cool steel countertop. Reaching forward, she unscrewed the blender lid and lifted the pitcher high above her face until she could pour water into her mouth. The water splashed from her mouth onto her cotton muscle shirt and pooled on the counter.

June glanced down at herself and chuckled softly. As her thirst abated, she noted her sweat-stained T-shirt, the waterlogged tea towels and her discarded clothing on the linoleum floor. In a burst of renewed energy, she twisted her legs free from the blender and hopped down from her shelf. The laundry was gathered quickly into a large plastic basket. June stepped back into her coveralls although their rubber lining chafed her damp skin.

Once in the apartment-complex laundry room, she was again bored and disappointed. The single washer was already occupied by a lone woman who sat on top of the machine, obviously preoccupied with a portable video game. June watched her idly. A final dribble of water drained into a wash tub as the machine lurched and clicked into its final cycle. The washer began to agitate. June sat on a rickety plastic chair with her laundry basket and glanced up at the sound. She observed more closely now the woman seated atop the washer. She wondered about the triangle of perspiration on her T-shirt and the white-knuckled grip on the edges of the vid screen. June strained forward to listen. Beneath the hum of the spin cycle, an uneven pulse was audible. Obviously not an EARTH-HOME appliance, she thought. And, then, she understood. Her laundry basket dropped from her lap onto the tiled floor. The woman atop the washer was rocking in time with the spin cycle. The washer had become unbalanced. Watching the woman on the tilting machine, June knew she must have her own top-loading washer.

Barbara Gowdy

We So Seldom Look On Love

WHEN YOU DIE, AND YOUR EARTHLY SELF BEGINS TURNING INTO YOUR disintegrated self, you radiate an intense current of energy. There is always energy given off when a thing turns into its opposite, when love, for instance, turns into hate. There are always sparks at those extreme points. But life turning into death is the most extreme of extreme points. So just after you die, the sparks are really stupendous. Really magical and explosive.

I've seen cadavers shining like stars. I'm the only person I've ever heard of who has. Almost everyone senses something, though, some vitality. That's why you get resistance to the idea of cremation or organ donation. "I want to be in one piece," people say. Even Matt, who claimed there was no soul and no afterlife, wrote a P.S. in his suicide note that he be buried intact.

As if it would have made any difference to his energy emission. No matter what you do— slice open the flesh, dissect everything, burn everything—you're in the path of a power beyond your little interferences.

I grew up in a nice, normal, happy family outside a small town in New Jersey. My parents and my brother are still living there. My Dad owned a flower store. Now my brother owns it. My brother is three years older than I am, a serious, remote man. But loyal. When I made the headlines, he phoned to say that if I needed money for a lawyer, he would give it to me. I was really touched. Especially as he was standing up to Carol, his wife. She got on the extension and screamed, "You're sick! You should be put away!"

She'd been wanting to tell me that since we were thirteen years old.

I had an animal cemetery back then. Our house was beside a woods and we had three outdoor cats, great hunters who tended to leave their kills in one piece. Whenever I found a body, usually a mouse or a bird, I took it into my bedroom and hid it until midnight. I didn't know anything about the ritual significance of the midnight hour. My burials took place then because that's when I woke up. It no longer happens, but I was such a sensitive child that I think I must have been aroused by the energy given off as day clicked over into the dead of night and, simultaneously, as the dead of night clicked over into the next day.

In any case, I'd be wide awake. I'd get up and go to the bathroom to wrap the body in toilet paper. I felt compelled to be so careful, so respectful. I whispered a chant. At each step on the burial I chanted. "I shroud the body, shroud the body, shroud little sparrow with broken wing." Or "I lower the body, lower the body ..." And so on.

Climbing out the bathroom window was accomplished by: "I enter the night, enter the night ..." At my cemetery I set the body down on a special flat rock and took my pyjamas off. I was behaving out of pure inclination. I dug up four or five graves and unwrapped the animals from their shrouds. The rotting smell was crucial. So was the cool air. Normally I'd be so keyed up at this point that I'd burst into a dance.

I used to dance for dead men, too. Before I climbed on top of them, I'd dance all around the prep room. When I told Matt about this he said that I was shaking my personality out of my body so that the sensation of participating in the cadaver's energy eruption would be intensified. "You're trying to imitate the disintegration process," he said.

Maybe—on an unconscious level. But what I was aware of was the heat, the heat of my danced-out body, which I cooled by lying on top of the cadavers. As a child I'd gently wipe my skin with two of the animals I'd just unwrapped. When I was covered all over with their scent, I put them aside, unwrapped the new corpse and did the same with it. I called this the Anointment. I can't describe how it felt. The high, high rapture. The electricity that shot through me.

The rest, wrapping the bodies back up and burying them, was pretty much what you'd expect.

It astonishes me now to think how naïve I was. I thought I had discovered something that certain other people, if they weren't afraid to give it a try, would find just as fantastic as I did. It was a dark and forbidden thing, yes, but so was sex. I really had no idea that I was jumping across a vast behavioural gulf. In fact, I couldn't see that I was doing anything wrong. I still can't, and I'm including what happened with Matt. Carol said I should have been put away, but I'm not bad-looking, so if offering my body to dead men is a crime, I'd like to know who the victim is.

Carol has always been jealous of me. She's fat and has a wandering eye. Her eye gives her a dreamy, distracted quality that I fell for (as I suppose my brother would eventually do) one day at a friend's thirteenth birthday party. It was the beginning of the summer holidays, and I was yearning for a kindred spirit, someone to share my secret life with. I saw Carol standing alone, looking everywhere at once, and I chose her.

I knew to take it easy, though. I knew not to push anything. We'd search for dead animals and birds, we'd chant and swaddle the bodies, dig graves, make Popsicle-stick crosses. All by daylight. At midnight I'd go out and dig up the grave and conduct a proper burial.

There must have been some chipmunk sickness that summer. Carol and I found an incredible number of chipmunks, and a lot of them had no blood on them, no sign of cat. One day we found a chipmunk that evacuated a string of foetuses when I picked it up. The foetuses were still alive, but there was no saving them, so I took them into the house and flushed them down the toilet.

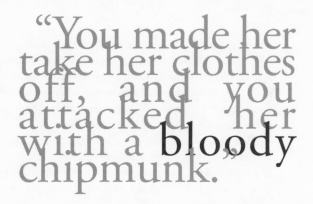

"You made her take her clothes off, and you attacked her with a bloody chipmunk."

A mighty force was coming from the mother chipmunk. It was as if, along with her own energy, she was discharging all the energy of her dead brood. When Carol and I began to dance for her, we both went a little crazy. We stripped to our underwear, screamed, spun in circles, threw dirt up into the air. Carol has always denied it, but she took off her bra and began whipping trees with it. I'm sure the sight of her doing this is what inspired me to take off my undershirt and underpants and to perform the Anointment.

Carol stopped dancing. I looked at her, and the expression on her face stopped me dancing, too. I looked down at the chipmunk in my hand. It was bloody. There were streaks of blood all over my body. I was horrified. I thought I'd squeezed the chipmunk too hard.

But what had happened was, I'd begun my period. I figured this out a few minutes after Carol ran off. I wrapped the chipmunk in its shroud and buried it. Then I got dressed and lay down on the grass. A little while later my mother appeared over me.

"Carol's mother phoned," she said. "Carol is very upset. She says you made her perform some disgusting witchcraft dance. You made her take her clothes off, and you attacked her with a bloody chipmunk."

"That's a lie," I said. "I'm menstruating."

After my mother had fixed me up with a sanitary napkin, she told me she didn't think I should play with Carol any more. "There's a screw loose in there somewhere," she said.

I had no intention of playing with Carol any more, but I cried at what seemed like a cruel loss. I think I knew that it was all loneliness from that moment on. Even though I was only thirteen, I was cutting any lines that still drifted out toward normal eroticism. Bosom friends, crushes, pyjama-party intimacy, I was cutting all those lines off.

A month or so after becoming a woman I developed a craving to perform autopsies. I resisted doing it for almost a year, though. I was frightened. Violating the intactness of the animal seemed sacrilegious and dangerous. Also unimaginable—I couldn't imagine what would happen.

Nothing. Nothing would happen, as I found out. I've read that necrophiles are frightened of getting hurt by normal sexual relationships, and maybe there's some truth in that (although my heart's been broken plenty of times by cadavers, and not once by a live man), but I think that my attraction to cadavers isn't driven by fear, it's driven by excitement, and that one of the most exciting things about a cadaver is how dedicated it is to dying. Its will is all directed to a single intention, like a huge wave heading for shore, and you can ride along on the wave if you want to, because no matter what you do, because with you or without you, that wave is going to hit the beach.

I felt this impetus the first time I worked up enough nerve to cut open a mouse. Like anyone else, I balked a little at slicing into the flesh, and I was repelled for a few seconds when I saw the insides. But something drove me to go through these compunctions. It was as if I were acting solely on instinct and curiosity, and anything I did was all right, provided it didn't kill me.

After the first few times, I started sticking my tongue into the incision. I don't know why. I thought about it, I did it, and I kept on doing it. One day I removed the organs and cleaned them with water, then put them back in, and I kept on doing that, too. Again, I couldn't tell you why except to say that any provocative thought, if you act upon it, seems to set you on a trajectory.

By the time I was sixteen I wanted human corpses. Men. (That way I'm straight.) I got my chauffeur's licence, but I had to wait until I had finished high school before Mr. Wallis would hire me as a hearse driver at the funeral home.

Mr. Wallis knew me because he bought bereavement flowers at my father's store. Now there was a weird man. He would take a trocar, which is the big needle you use to draw out a cadaver's fluids, and he would push it up the penises of dead men to make them look semi-erect, and then he'd sodomize them. I caught him at it once, and he tried to tell me that he'd been urinating in the hopper. I pretended to believe him. I was upset though, because I knew that dead men were just dead flesh to him. One minute he'd be locked up with a young male corpse, having his way with him, and the next he'd be embalming him as if nothing had happened, and making sick jokes about him, pretending to find evidence of rampant homosexuality—colons stalagmited with dried semen, and so on.

None of this joking ever happened in front of me. I heard about it from the crazy old man who did the mopping up. He was also a necrophile, I'm almost certain, but no longer active. He called dead women Madonnas. He rhapsodized about the beautiful Madonnas he'd had the privilege of seeing in the 1940s, about how much more womanly and feminine the Madonnas were twenty years before.

I just listened. I never let on what I was feeling, and I don't think anyone suspected. Necrophiles aren't supposed to be blond and pretty, let alone female. When I'd been working at the funeral home for about a year, a committee from the town council tried to get me to enter the Milk Marketer's Beauty Pageant. They knew about my job, and they knew I was studying embalming at night, but I had told people I was preparing myself for medical school, and I guess the council believed me.

After leaving his place I'd gone straight to the funeral home and made love to an **autopsy case.**

For fifteen years, ever since Matt died, people have been asking me how a woman makes love to a corpse.

Matt was the only person who figured it out. He was a medical student, so he knew that if you apply pressure to the chest of certain fresh corpses, they purge blood out of their mouths.

Matt was smart. I wish I could have loved him with more than sisterly love. He was tall and thin. My type. We met at the doughnut shop across from the medical library, got to talking, and liked each other immediately, an unusual experience for both of us. After about an hour I knew that he loved me and that his love was unconditional. When I told him where I worked and what I was studying, he asked why.

"Because I'm a necrophile," I said.

He lifted his head and stared at me. He had eyes like high-resolution monitors. Almost too vivid. Normally I don't like looking people in the eye, but I found myself staring back. I could see that he believed me.

"I've never told anyone else," I said.

"With men or women?" he asked.

"Men. Young men."

"How?"

"Cunnilingus."

"Fresh corpses?"

"If I can get them."

"What do you do, climb on top of them?"

"Yes."

"You're turned on by blood."

"It's a lubricant," I said. "It's colourful. Stimulating. It's the ultimate bodily fluid."

"Yes," he said, nodding. "When you think about it. Sperm propagates life. But blood sustains it. Blood is primary."

He kept asking questions, and I answered them as truthfully as I could. Having confessed what I was, I felt myself driven to test his intellectual rigour and the strength of his love at first sight. Throwing rocks at him without any expectation that he'd stay standing. He did, though. He caught the whole arsenal and asked for more. It began to excite me.

We went back to his place. He had a basement apartment in an old rundown building. There were books in orange-crate shelves, in piles on the floor, all over the bed. On the wall above his desk was a poster of Doris Day in the movie *Tea for Two*. Matt said she looked like me.

"Do you want to dance first?" he asked, heading for his record player. I'd told him about how I danced before climbing on corpses.

"No."

He swept the books off the bed. Then he undressed me. He had an erection until I told him I was a virgin. "Don't worry," he said, sliding his head down my stomach. "Lie still."

The next morning he phoned me at work. I was hungover and blue from the night before. After leaving his place I'd gone straight to the funeral home and made love to an autopsy case. Then I'd got drunk in a seedy country-and-western bar and debated going back to the funeral home and suctioning out my blood until I lost consciousness.

It had finally hit me that I was incapable of falling in love with a man who wasn't dead. I kept thinking, "I'm not normal." I'd never faced this before. Obviously, making love to a corpse isn't normal, but while I was still a virgin I must have been assuming that I could give it up any time I liked. Get married, have babies. I must have been banking on a future that I didn't even want let alone have access to.

Matt was phoning to get me to come around again after work.

"I don't know," I said.

"You had a good time. Didn't you?"

"Sure, I guess."

"I think you're fascinating," he said.

I sighed.

"Please," he said. "Please."

A few nights later I went to his apartment. From then on we started to meet every Tuesday and Thursday evening after my embalming class, and as soon as I left his place, if I knew there was a corpse at the mortuary—any male corpse, young or old—I went straight there and climbed in a basement window.

Entering the prep room, especially at night when there was nobody else around, was like diving into a lake. Sudden cold and silence, and the sensation of penetrating a new element where the rules of other elements don't apply. Being with Matt was like lying on the beach of the lake. Matt had warm, dry skin. His apartment was overheated and noisy. I lay on Matt's bed and soaked him up, but only to make the moment when I entered the prep room even more overpowering.

If the cadaver was freshly embalmed, I could usually smell him from the basement. The smell is like a hospital and old cheese. For me, it's the smell of danger and permission, it used to key me up like amphetamine, so that by the time I reached the prep room, tremors were running up and down my legs. I locked the door behind me and broke into a wild dance, tearing my clothes off, spinning around, pulling at my hair. I'm not sure what this was all about, whether or not I was trying to take part in the chaos of the corpse's disintegration, as Matt suggested. Maybe I was prostrating myself, I don't know.

Once the dancing was over I was always very calm, almost entranced. I drew back the sheet. This was the most exquisite moment. I felt as if I were being blasted by white light. Almost blinded, I climbed onto the table and straddled the corpse. I ran my hands over his skin. My hands and the insides of my thighs burned as if I were touching dry ice. After a few minutes I lay down and pulled the sheet up over my head. I began to kiss his mouth. By now he might be drooling blood. A corpse's blood is thick, cool and sweet. My head roared.

I was no longer depressed. Far from it, I felt better, more confident, than I had ever felt in my life. I had discovered myself to be irredeemably abnormal. I could either slit my throat or surrender—wholeheartedly now—to my obsession. I surrendered. And what happened was that obsession began to storm through me, as if I were a tunnel. I became the medium of obsession as well as both ends of it. With Matt, when we made love, I was the receiving end, I was the cadaver. When I left him and went to the funeral home, I was the lover. Through me Matt's love poured into the cadavers at the funeral home, and through me the cadavers filled Matt with explosive energy.

He quickly got addicted to this energy. The minute I arrived at his apartment, he had to hear every detail about the last corpse I'd been with. For a month or so I had him pegged as a latent homosexual necrophile voyeur, but then I began to see that it wasn't the corpses themselves that excited him, it was my passion for them. It was the power that went into that passion and that came back, doubled, for his pleasure. He kept asking, "How do you feel? Why do you think you felt that way?" And then, because the source of all this power disturbed him, he'd try to prove that my feelings were delusory.

"A corpse shows simultaneous extremes of character," I told him. "Wisdom and innocence, happiness and grief, and so on."

"Therefore all corpses are alike," he said. "Once you've had one you've had them all."

"No, no. They're all different. Each corpse contains his own extremes. Each corpse is only as wise and as innocent as the living person could have been."

He said, "You're drafting personalities onto corpses in order to have power over them."

"In that case," I said, "I'm pretty imaginative, since I've never met two corpses who were alike."

"You *could* be that imaginative," he argued. "Schizophrenics are capable of manufacturing dozens of complex personalities."

I didn't mind these attacks. There was no malice in them, and there was no way they could touch me, either. It was as if I were luxuriously pouring my heart out to a very clever, very concerned, very tormented analyst. I felt sorry for him. I understood his twisted desire to turn me into somebody else (somebody who might love him). I used to fall madly in love with cadavers and then cry because they were dead. The difference between Matt and me was that I had become philosophical. I was all right.

I thought that he was, too. He was in pain, yes, but he seemed confident that what he was going through was temporary and not unnatural. "I am excessively curious," he said. "My fascination is any curious man's fascination with the unusual."

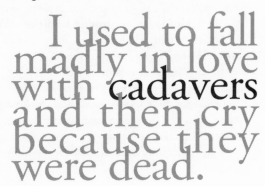

I used to fall madly in love with **cadavers** and then cry because they were dead.

He said that by feeding his lust through mine, he would eventually saturate it, then turn it to disgust.

I told him to go ahead, give it a try. So he began to scour the newspapers for my cadavers' obituaries and to go to their funerals and memorial services. He made charts of my preferences and the frequency of my morgue encounters. He followed me to the morgue at night and waited outside so that he could get a replay while I was still in an erotic haze. He sniffed my skin. He pulled me over to streetlights and examined the blood on my face and hands.

I suppose I shouldn't have encouraged him. I can't really say why I did, except that in the beginning I saw his obsession as the outer edge of my own obsession, a place I didn't have to visit as long as he was there. And then later, and despite his increasingly erratic behaviour, I started to have doubts about an obsession that could come on so suddenly and that could come through me.

One night he announced that he might as well face it, he was going to have to make love to corpses, male corpses. The idea nauseated him, he said, but he said that secretly, deep down, unknown even to himself, making love to male corpses was clearly the target of his desire. I blew up. I told him that necrophilia wasn't something you forced yourself to do. You longed to do it, you needed to do it. You were born to do it.

He wasn't listening. He was glued to the dresser mirror. In the last weeks of his life he stared at himself in the mirror without the least self-consciousness. He focused on his face, even though what was going on from the neck down was the arresting part. He had begun to wear incredibly weird outfits. Velvet capes, pantaloons, high-heeled red boots. When we made love, he kept these outfits on. He stared into my eyes, riveted (it later occurred to me) by his own reflection.

Matt committed suicide, there was never any doubt about that. As for the necrophilia, it wasn't a crime, not fifteen years ago. So even though I was caught in the act, naked and straddling an unmistakably dead body, even though the newspapers found out about it and made it front-page news, there was nothing the police could charge me with.

In spite of which I made a full confession. It was crucial to me that the official report contain more than the detective's bleak observations. I wanted two things on record: one, that Matt was ravished by a reverential expert; two, that his cadaver blasted the energy of a star.

"Did this energy blast happen before or after he died?" the detective asked.

"After," I said, adding quickly that I couldn't have foreseen such a blast. The one tricky area was why I hadn't stopped the suicide. Why I hadn't talked, or cut, Matt down.

I lied. I said that as soon as I entered Matt's room, he kicked away the ladder. Nobody could prove otherwise. But I've often wondered how much time actually passed between when I opened the door and when his neck broke. In crises, a minute isn't a minute. There's the same chaos you get at the instant of death, with time and form breaking free, and everything magnifying and coming apart.

Matt must have been in a state of crisis for days, maybe weeks before he died. All that

True obses-
sion depends
on the object's
absolute un-
responsiveness.

staring in mirrors, thinking, "Is this my face?" Watching as his face separated into its infinitesimal particles and reassembled into a strange new face. The night before he died, he had a mask on. A Dracula mask, but he wasn't joking. He wanted to wear the mask while I made love to him as if he were a cadaver. No way, I said. The whole point, I reminded him, was that I played the cadaver. He begged me, and I laughed because of the mask and with relief. If he wanted to turn the game around, then it was over between us, and I was suddenly aware of how much I liked that idea.

The next night he phoned me at my parents' and said, "I love you," then hung up.

I don't know how I knew, but I did. A gun, I thought. Men always use guns. And then I thought, no, poison, cyanide. He was a medical student and had access to drugs. When I arrived at his apartment, the door was open. Across from the door, taped to the wall, was a note: "DEAD PERSON IN BEDROOM."

But he wasn't dead. He was standing on a step-ladder. He was naked. An impressively knotted noose, attached to a pipe that ran across the ceiling, was looped around his neck.

He smiled tenderly. "I knew you'd come," he said.

"So why the note?" I demanded.

"Pull away the ladder," he crooned. "My beloved."

"Come on. This is stupid. Get down." I went up to him and punched his leg.

"All you have to do," he said, "is pull away the ladder."

His eyes were even darker and more expressive than usual. His cheekbones appeared to be highlighted. (I discovered minutes later he had make-up on.) I glanced around the room for a chair or a table that I could bring over and stand on. I was going to take the noose off him myself.

"If you leave," he said, "if you take a step back, if you do anything other than pull away the ladder, I'll kick it away."

"I love you," I said. "Okay?"

"No, you don't," he said.

"I do!" To sound like I meant it I stared at his legs and imagined them lifeless. "I do!"

"No, you don't," he said softly. "But," he said, "you will."

I was gripping the ladder. I remember thinking that if I held tight to the ladder, he wouldn't be able to kick it away. I was gripping the ladder, and then it was by the wall, tipped over. I have no memory of the transition between these two events. There was a loud crack, and gushing water. Matt dropped gracefully, like a girl fainting. Water poured on him from the broken pipe. There was a smell of excrement. I dragged him by the noose.

In the living room I pulled him onto the green shag carpet. I took my clothes off. I knelt over him. I kissed the blood at the corner of his mouth.

True obsession depends on the object's absolute unresponsiveness. When I used to fall for a particular cadaver, I would feel as if I were a hollow instrument, a bell or a flute. I'd empty out. *I* would clear out (it was involuntary) until I was an instrument for the cadaver to swell into and be amplified. As the object of Matt's obsession how could I be other than impassive, while he was alive?

He was playing with fire, playing with me. Not just because I couldn't love him, but because I was irradiated. The whole time that I was involved with Matt, I was making love to corpses, absorbing their energy, blazing it back out. Since that energy came from the act of life alchemizing into death, there's a possibility that it was alchemical itself. Even if it wasn't, I'm sure it gave Matt the impression that I had the power to change him in some huge and dangerous way.

I now believe that his addiction to my energy was really a craving for such a transformation. In fact, I think that all desire is desire for transformation, and that all transformation—all movement, all process—happens because life turns into death.

I am still a necrophile, occasionally, and recklessly. I have found no replacement for the torrid serenity of a cadaver.

BET THAT'S MY PROBLEM.. NO WONDER I'VE BEEN KINDA EDGY LATELY... SHIT, MY ARMS HURT... I'M HUNGRY... I'LL FIX SOMETHING SOON AS I PUT THE GROCERIES AWAY

UNGH! GRUNT GASP GASP GRUNT UUUGHHHH AAAGGG GASP UNGHHHH GRUNT

GUESS I'M THROUGH PUTTING THE GROCERIES AWAY...

SWM, 23...GWM... SWF.... DWM, 35, SEEKS SLENDER... SWF... SWM, 42, 5'9, 240LBS... SWM, 20... DWM, 54... DWF... DWM, 41, LOOKING FOR PETITE... SBM... SWM, 34, JEWISH... SWF... SWM, 39, INTO HIKING... SBF... LESBIAN... SWF... SWF... DWM, 41, TALL, VEGETARIAN... SWM, 43, PISCES... DWM, PROF; FINANCIAL SECURE, 62... SWM, 37, NS, INTELLIGENT, W/HERPES... SBM... SWM, 25... LESBIAN... SBF... GWM... SWM, 40, CHRISTIAN SWM, 36, NS, BALDING... SWM SEEKS ATHLETIC... DWF BI... SWM, 37, SEEKS FIT... DWM, 32, OUTGOING, CHEERFUL SWM, 39, PROF, SEEKS LADY, 25-40 WHO WANTS CHILDREN... SWF... SBM... WWM, 42, NS, SPIRITUAL... GWM... SWM, SEEKS FUN-LOVING... DWF... DBM... SUCCESSFUL HANDSOME JEWISH... SWM 36, ARTIST... SWF... DWF... SWM, 40 SEEKS SLENDER... SBM... DWM, SEEKING SWF, 30'S, VIVACIOUS... SWM, 23...

95% BRAN FLAKES

...FINANCIALLY SECURE... HEY, THIS GUY SOUNDS OKAY... AND IT SOUNDS LIKE HE'S GOT SOME BUCKS... AND, HE MUST BE PRETTY DESPERATE, OR HE WOULDN'T HAVE AN AD IN HERE...

HOT MEN 976-DICK

OF COURSE, IF I ANSWER THIS, IT PROBABLY MEANS I'M DESPERATE, TOO... NAHH... IT'S WORSE IF YOU HAVE TO PAY FOR ONE OF THESE EXPENSIVE ADS... IT ONLY COSTS ME A STAMP... WHAT IF THE GUY'S A PSYCHO, OR SOMETHING... HECK, I CAN ALWAYS GET MY PHONE NUMBER CHANGED IF HE STARTS CALLING AND HARASSING ME OR SOME...

BET HE WON'T CALL... THIS WAS A STUPID THING TO DO... WASTE ALL THAT TIME AND A PERFECTLY GOOD STAMP... AND IF HE DOES CALL, HE'S PROBABLY GONNA BE SOME SORT OF A WEIRDO OR A RELIGIOUS NUT OR...

US MAIL

ONE WEEK LATER...

SBM... DWM, 42, 5'10, 210 LB.
GWM... SWF... SWM, 34, NS,
CHRISTIAN... HEY, HERE'S
THE SAME AD FROM THAT GUY
I WROTE TO... HE NEVER
GOT BACK TO ME... STUPID
JERK... I PROBABLY DIDN'T
SOUND SKINNY ENOUGH... OR
MAYBE HE WAS SOME SORT
OF NUT CASE... I OUGHT TO BE
GLAD HE DIDN'T...

H--HELLO--? OH--- UMM...
YES... YES IT IS...
--- OH.. UMM.-- SURE.-
UMM.-- WELL, I, UM, LIKED
YOUR AD, too-- UMM..
-- OH --UM-- YES...
THAT SOUNDS NICE...
SOMETIME--

..TONIGHT?... WELL, I
HAVE TO GET UP EARLY
TOMORROW.-- THAT WOULD
BE **BETTER**.. YES...
DINNER SOUNDS NICE...
.. OKAY... OKAY...

I'VE GOT A...
DATE TOMORROW
NIGHT...

.. **SHIT!**

WONDER IF THE GREEN DRESS STILL FITS...
BUT THE BROWN SHOES DON'T GO WITH IT.
THE RESTAURANTS DOWNTOWN... KIND OF A
CRAPPY AREA... AND THERE WON'T BE ANY
PARKING.-- MEXICAN FOOD... SHIT, I
WONDER IF HE'S A MEXICAN... PAUL...
SHIT... I'LL PROBABLY GET THE FARTS
FROM IT... OR AT LEAST ALL BLOATED...

HE'LL PROBABLY TRY TO GET HIS HANDS ALL OVER ME
--- PROBABLY THINKS I'M SOME KIND OF A SLUT CAUSE
I ANSWERED AN AD... OR HE'LL THINK I'M REALLY
DESPERATE

THIS IS RIDICULOUS.--
THE GUY'S PROBABLY
A..**TOAD**... OR
HE'S REALLY MARRIED
OR HE'S PSYCHO..
I'LL PROBABLY
GET THE SHITS
IF I EAT ANY
HOT SAUCE ...

Xaviera Hollander
The Three-Way

This text is transcribed from Hollander's album
Xaviera!, *which was released in the early 1970s
with GRT of Canada Limited. On this album
Hollander explains, in a number of monologues,
her sexual philosophies and her views on men
and "hookers"; the record also contains one-act
dramas in which Hollander and various part-
ners act out sex-scenarios. The following scenario
involves Xaviera and a married couple.*

[*Traffic noise*]

MALE VOICE
Excuse me, Miss Hollander?

XAVIERA
Yes, what can I do for you? What are you
waiting outside here for?

MALE VOICE
Well we're just, uh, we heard you on the
radio, my wife and I—

[*Xaviera laughs*]

Sharon over here …

XAVIERA
She's a lovely lady. What's your name?
Sharon?

SHARON
Sharon, yeah.

XAVIERA
And what's your name?

MALE VOICE
Bill.

XAVIERA
Uh-huh. Why don't we go out for a drink? I
think you look like a groovy couple.

SHARON
Oh that would be nice.

BILL
That, that'd be wonderful.

XAVIERA
Can you just open the door and let me in?

[*More traffic noise, sound of car door opening*]

SHARON
Here I'll get in the ... you sit up front.

XAVIERA
[*laughs*] Okay, can you trust me? Do you think you can trust me?

[*Swanky music begins in background*]

Let's go up to my place, because I've had a tiring day of being on the radio a few hours, with all those nasty little ladies calling. Go straight ahead, and it's the third street to your right, and then to the left, and I'll tell you while we're driving. Just go ahead, okay?

[*Music interlude with traffic noises*]

Okay, just two more blocks and we're there. [*traffic. Music continues*] There it is. Let's park.

SHARON
This is nice, it's a nice building.

XAVIERA
Yeah, it's not the best, but I'm in the process of trying to settle down somewhere. It's on the seventh floor. Let's go up and have some fun. [*laughs*] I'm right in the mood today, I, you know ...

SHARON
We just don't do things like this, you know, but I, we really wanted to, to meet you, well we've never met a celebrity before, and well, you're really nice!

XAVIERA
I still prefer to walk around in blue jeans and a sweater without a bra on and no make-up, but somehow I've got to live up to the sex image, the sex-symbol image. Do you mind if I change my dress, and take my stockings off and just put a little easy peignoir on?

SHARON
Oh, no ...

XAVIERA
I won't shock or offend you, would I?

BILL
Oh no, no.

XAVIERA
I hope the contrary. [*laughs*] Let me just put a nice record on the background. Billy, you be the bartender, I'll go inside.

[*Soft, mellow music plays*]

SHARON
I can't believe we really came here! It's nice, isn't it?

BILL
[*whispers*] Yeah.

SHARON
[*sotto voce*] Are you going to ask her?

BILL
Sure ... want a drink?

SHARON
Um, yeah, yeah, I want a drink, a double ... that's enough, that's enough.

XAVIERA
[*returning into room*] Oh that was great! I feel
like a new-born baby. You should feel my
skin, I feel so soft all over. Have you ever visited a hooker, paid a visit to a hooker?

SHARON
It's all right Bill.

BILL
Well, I might as well be honest ...

SHARON
Yes?

XAVIERA
Just be honest about it!

BILL
Well yes I have, as a matter of fact.

SHARON
When?

XAVIERA
Oh don't get nasty now, don't get nasty. You
know, he confessed it, just let him do his
thing. Did you like it, or what did you think
of the hooker?

BILL
Yeah, I, I liked it. There was something,
maybe experienced about it, that, uh, maybe
she's lacking sometimes.

SHARON
That's, that's sort of our problem, um, well
Bill just doesn't seem to think that I turn him
on any more. I would really like to, but I really
just don't know how.

XAVIERA
She's such a lovely woman, you know. You
have such a sensuous mouth ...

BILL
Well she's very attractive.

XAVIERA
Yeah, you are.

BILL
Her mouth, I'd like her to do more with her
mouth.

XAVIERA
Yeah, that's it, you've got a mouth that is
shaped for sucking, really! Don't be shocked
now, that's it, you know, too many women
are embarrassed about it, if the man, most
men who go to hookers, and let me tell you
a little story about it, most men who come
to hookers, the first thing they want is a blow
job, really, is oral sex, fellatio. And when you
ask them why, they tell you because my wife
doesn't want to do it, my wife doesn't feel
like it, she thinks it's dirty, it's degrading, she
says, "What do you think I am, I'm not a
whore." But oral sex, and this might well
account for you, young man—as well as you,
young lady—is a matter of learning. It's also
a matter of techniques, it's not only a matter
of putting your mouth on the spot. Now—
instead of just talking here, with our clothes
on, you know, I'm getting turned on thinking about the subject, why don't you take
your drink, and, you know, since you both
wanted to meet me, I guess you wouldn't have
any objections if you make me too. [*breathy
laugh*] Or rather, vice versa, I'd love to make
it with both of you—let's go to the bedroom.

SHARON
[*with trembling voice*] Well it's all right, if you and Bill want to go ahead …

XAVIERA
[*angrily*] Oh don't be so puritanical! Not me and Bill! Bill obviously knows what it's about, but it's really you that needs the straightening out.

SHARON
Well, all right …

XAVIERA
Bill, you know, you've read the books. I dig ladies, I really do, she's a beautiful woman. I'd almost be jealous of you, young man! [*Bill laughs nervously*] Don't you like to watch two women making love?

BILL
Oh, Do I like to watch?

XAVIERA
Yeah.

BILL
Yes, yes, as a matter of fact I do.

XAVIERA
Turns a lot of men on. Take off your clothes, take off that lovely purple sweater of yours and those long pants.

BILL
Aren't you getting undressed?

XAVIERA
I have only one peignoir, all I've got to do is take it all off. I've got nothing underneath. Put your hand here, put it right on my belly,

[*sighs*] put it up higher … mmmm …

BILL
My word.

SHARON
How do we go about this, I mean who, who starts?

XAVIERA
Who does who?

[*General laughter*]

All right, uh, okay, I'll just kneel on my knees behind the bed. Give me your big toe, let me suck your toe … You see that Sharon? I bet you've never sucked your husband's toe.

SHARON
No, I've never *seen* that before!

XAVIERA
You've never seen anybody suck a toe … do you like it?

BILL
It does feel very good.

SHARON
[*incredulous*] It does?

XAVIERA
Isn't it like I'm sucking your organ?

BILL
Well I'm hoping you'll get there.

XAVIERA
No, but doesn't it feel like it, just [*sucking noise*] with my mouth on top of it … Why don't

you take off your bra and your underpanties? I dig women. If they're nice and they turn me on, they turn me on all the way and I don't need a man right now, so take yourself at hand and just let me take care of your wife.
[*The sound of Bill's masturbation is heard in the background at this point, and continues ...*]

Let me kiss you, those sensuous lips ...

SHARON
Kiss me?

XAVIERA
Yes, open your mouth, put your tongue inside my tongue.

[*Sighing, kissing noises and groans are audible*]

Spread your legs a bit, Sharon.

SHARON
Well ...

XAVIERA
Don't be uptight ...

SHARON
Well ...

XAVIERA
Please, you are clean, you're beautiful, you're gorgeous.

SHARON
Oh, all right.

XAVIERA
Put your legs apart ... I want to have your nectar. [*mutual sighs*] You like that? I know how to find that clitoris. Let me spread it

open, oh, feel, let's all touch and feel ...
[*Moaning, sighing interlude*]

XAVIERA
Now I'm ... you know what? Turn around. So that you can eat—you can come close to my triangle. It's hot and passionate and waiting with desire for you.

SHARON
All right.

XAVIERA
I bet you've never even touched a woman, have you?

SHARON
No, I haven't. [*laughs*] This is really, this is great!

BILL
Do you think it's bizarre?

SHARON
Yes, but I like it!

XAVIERA
Sharon, come close to me.

SHARON
Okay.

XAVIERA
You see his penis?

SHARON
Yes.

XAVIERA
All right, now I put my mouth around the head of his penis ...

[*Sharon murmurs assent*]

... and put it all the way deep, over his shaft—you've got to move your tongue, move your tongue around the head, right there where his skin starts you know...

SHARON
Oh ...

XAVIERA
... and just move it, flick it around, left and right, and mouth over it again. And now meanwhile, with your other hand—here you do it, with your hand while I'm sucking him. You caress his balls ...

SHARON
Mmmm ...

XAVIERA
... and the bridge in between his arse and his balls ...

[*Interlude of fellatio, involving Sharon's and Xaviera's handiwork, and Bill's moaning. Bill climaxes, loudly, Sharon says "Wow!" Sighs all around*]

I've had my vitamins for the day! [*laughs*] Oh, you're beautiful!

BILL
I've stopped again.

XAVIERA
[*laughs*] Oh, you're young, and I'm sure ...

SHARON
Bill, I really didn't know you had it in you.

XAVIERA
[*laughter*] I envy you men. I have got one terrific sexual fantasy, and it is to have a huge dick. [*sighs*] I would put it right inside you ...

SHARON
Do you ever use one of those things, what are they called?

XAVIERA
Dildoes.

SHARON
Oh, yeah?

XAVIERA
Do you want one, I have one. I have a double dildo! How about the double dildo?

SHARON
It's something, isn't it?

XAVIERA
It's huge, it's something else, it's bigger than you, I want you to know.

[*Sharon and Xaviera begin to employ the double dildo, accompanied by noises of ecstasy*]

XAVIERA
Deeper, deeper ... hold me, caress my nipples, squeeze my nipples, Bill, you too. Oh, just get in the action ... ooooooh!

[*Sharon and Xaviera cry out and moan as they begin to climax, Bill murmurs something suspiciously, about Sharon trying "not to come," but they both climax, uproariously*]

XAVIERA
[*over Sharon's cries*] Look at her nipples!
They're standing up like cherries!

BILL
I know.

XAVIERA
That's it, it was beautiful, wasn't it?

SHARON
Oh, it's been a long time.

BILL
It's going to be hard now, without you!
[*laughs, in worried way*]

XAVIERA
No, it's all right, you'll manage. I'll come by
one of these days and I'll see what progress
you've made.

SHARON
Well, I was going to ask when we could come
again.

Beth Brant

J.R.

EVEN NOW THE TEXTURE OF YOUR VOICE OVER THE PHONE COVERS ME WITH memory of your silk-brown skin, your nipples brushing my own, your tongue marking trails on my neck, my mouth, my shoulders.
Your breath in my ear—"Te'amo."

I told you then I would write poems to you.
Years later, I am writing this one.

The sound of your voice this night has carried me to the place of writing.
Something I could give you—years after our heated, rushed love, spanning only thirty days—the residue of those nights and days remains inside me like the scent from the passion-soaked sheets lingered in your room.
I spread my legs and my body to you. I spread my self to you, opening and opening to every touch and word you caressed on me. "Te'amo," you whispered. "Mi corazón," you sang.

Your fingers on my back as we danced, the brush of your hand on my arm as we rode the subway, the way you held a book, the way you danced the Salsa, the way you talked, the colour of your eyes—like black stones found in the sea; wet, beautiful, full of story. All these made heat rise in me.

Hot for you, wet for you.
My wetness; flowing, waiting to coat your fingers and hands, your lips and tongue.

Hot for you. Wet for you.

breath

Kissing me as you rose from my open thighs, I would taste the liquid of myself on your tongue.

You made tapes of Willie Colon, Luciecita, Armando Reyes—knowing I would never listen to this music again without remembering the humidity of your room—candles lit, flowers placed in front of the image of La Virgen, bowls of water and salt flanking her picture. The dish of sand from your beloved Puerto Rico, the rosary of your mother laid across the white cloth. Each day you placed bread upon this altar.

I watched your hands perform this act of love, then turned to receive your body in another act of love.

You asked me to run away with you to your island. I imagined your land as you wove the descriptions to me. I could smell the water surrounding your land as I touched your breasts. I could taste the fruits of your land as I put my fingers inside you, then licked the cream that poured from you.

I knew I would not run with you, but I imagined your land.
And told you I would write poems to you. *upon*

Poems that would detail our meeting:
"I only fall for women who have Scorpio rising," you joked.
"I have Scorpio rising," I said.
Your confident, loud laughter as you took my hand and kissed my life-line.
"Somehow, I knew that," and your lips burned the lines that mapped my palm.

Poems that would describe the Staten Island ferry, the restaurants we ate in, the New York stories, your neighbourhood of pimps and junkies tangling with new Yuppies who came to exorcise the streets.

Poems about the presents you gave me: the topaz earrings, the flowers, the ring from Guatemala, the Tarot cards, the silk blouse you bought because it was the colour of my eyes.
"A blue-eyed Indian," you sighed as you kissed my eyelids. "Tell me about this blue-eyed Indian."
And I told you secrets about myself. Secrets I knew you would keep.

Poems about the food you cooked for me. The sauce of garlic and oil that coated the platanos, yami, and chocho with an opaque sheen. The carne stews, the rice, the thick, black coffee you boiled on the stove, adding sugar and milk until it became a confection.

Poems about your political activism for Puerto Rican independence, your Marxist-feminist analysis of everything, the gentleness towards your sisters who were locked in prison and whom you visited as often as possible, carrying sweets and flowers that were inevitably confiscated. But you persevered and fought for the right of beauty in that ugly world.

Poems scented with the sweat underneath your large breasts, the liquid between your legs, the black curling hair of your cunt, the dark mauve of your clitoris before you came, the salty-sweetness of your back.

Poems about your tenderness and roughness, the glorious revelling in our sex, the love words, the sex words whispered between us—Spanish and English mingling like our smells— lush, humid, close in your magic room.

"Say it, say it," you whispered between my legs.

And I would speak with waves upon waves of orgasm, my body shaking and soaring into a land of tropical heat and dust-covered roads, canopies of trees, sounds of ocean lapping against sand.

I was going to write poems to you.
Years later there is this.

soft

Each day was going to be my last with you.

Your voice, heavy with sex, "Te'amo," and I would postpone the journey home.

I had come here when the air was still cold, snow falling outside Gloria's apartment, and too soon the trees in Central Park began leafing new green, the whores on Alphabet Street were shedding coats to better display their skinny bodies to customers, the junkies were nodding off in the sun.

It was not my intention to give anything up, especially myself.

Nor did I.

thighs

I had no intentions, no plans, no wishes.

Your call was fierce, sweet, and my answer mirrored your fierceness, matched your sweetness.

Our last night, the candles burning a hot, steady flame, you again touched every part of me that could bring pleasure. You held my face in your hands and licked the tears, a mixture of yours and mine.

"Women leave me. Why?"

Now, as we talk on the phone from time to time, your voice raised in outrage at the latest political atrocity, the latest homophobic attack, you recite the latest failed relationship— married women, straight women, unfaithful women.

Exasperated, I tell you that you only find what you are looking for, women who will leave you.

"You don't want a solid relationship," I say. "Only ones that will prove your ability to make a conquest."

"Si, querida," you say. "So, when are you coming to New York again?"

You laugh, and in my mind's eye, I see your full, dark lips drawn across your white even teeth, and I want to feel those lips on mine and on my body, sucking my breasts, sucking out the honeyed liquid that flows so readily at the sound of your voice.

I laugh with you.

"I have never made love with a grandmother," you say teasingly.

"You must be losing your touch."

"I haven't lost my touch, mi corazón. Perhaps you have just forgotten it."

I have not forgotten your touch. It comes to me at times I least expect—a gift from the conscious past—wrapped in brown silk and carrying the smell of botánicas where we purchased candles and magic herbs. I have not forgotten your touch.

We have seen each other through the years—at conferences, at seminars. I am always careful not to be alone with you, except in safe places like cafés. You send me birthday cards and presents each May. We talk on the phone, your calls coming during the day when you know I will be alone.

I keep your letters and cards in a special place, alongside the topaz earrings, the take-out menu from Ming Gardens, the dried roses from the bouquet you gave me at the airport on our last day in New York.

But even in the safety of cafés, your gestures and voice bring back memories of wet nights, wet bodies, wet places of love. The smell of you as you laboured to bring forth every sensation from my being. Reaching into my body for response, your hands entering all parts of me, you whisper, "Te'amo, te'amo. Speak to me, querida. Say it, say it."

I spoke in the language of my body.
The speech of my willing skin.
The dialect of my swollen nipples.
The accent of breath upon soft thighs.
The phrases of shouts and sighs of joy and release.

Years later, I give this poem to you.
It is small next to your abundance of spirit.
So generously you loved me.

I give this to you.
And you will know, querida, this is yet another way to say
"Te'amo."

Ellen Flanders • *Lesbian Peep Show: A Tragic Narrative*

i usually like dominant femmes

i'm a butch bottom

but she was an androgynous butch/femme top/bottom

i wanted to suck on her lip

i wanted to fuck her

i strutted like a butch top

i wanted her to fuck me

and acted coy like a bratty bottom

i watched through my confused gaze

and did nothing

Robyn Cakebread

27:will

t HE STREET. DARK, BUT FOR THE CORNER. LIGHTS GUIDE HER EYE UP THE HARD swelling of the street. she stands looking waiting. waiting for the one. she is numb. the summer night is hot and sticky. cars pass by. some slowly, others quickly. shadows pass by. they are not noticed. they are feared. they are all big. are all good. she wears a long cotton skirt. denim. a tank top. it makes her feel, sexy. she is hungry. hunger consumes her. she waits. stands hard, slumped. a hard embodiment of people. all the people she has known. this is her street. no one comes to her without invitation. she is tired. she is hungry. her hunger never leaves. the people are her salvation. her escape and her freedom. freedom to feel loved. freedom to feel nothing. her eyes are glazed. she never smiles, only when they come. a car, stops. she speaks. gets in. the lights are the safety. she counts. she talks. they pull into a driveway. she is hot. very hot. hungry. her heart races. she takes the offering. hides it. pulls up her long skirt. she is wet, desperate. she touches her hunger. the light is obscure. she looks down. leans, over. into the darkness. the clouds bob up and down in the park where she played. she sees his penis. hard, entombed. sounds around are slurred. she is very hungry. she needs to be fed to be loved. aches for love. she loves him. loves him loves. excitement rises in her throat. she hurts. cries out. consumes her meal. it slides inside her. throbs. she grips, pulls, rips, scratches. there is nothing. her hunger grows. blackness rips through her mind. she must get it. will die without it. on the corner. wet from the heat. loves to feel wet. she is the princess. is loved. the blackness hangs all around. the air moulds to her body. her hard body. a body she cannot feel. a body she displays. it is her art. she hates it. transforms it. easily. she is magical. she is many people. shadows speak. which is the prince. who has the magic. in a room. bed, table, kettle, pillow, blanket, chair. he loves her. she dances. under dark hair. over dull lines. undresses for her silk-brown man. arbitrary. he sits. he strokes. she stands. she caresses her new self. her hard body. standing, her hands move gently up her calves. legs spread. spins around. in the park where she played. she grips muscles behind her.

her legs are long. his breath comes in and then out, deeply. she bends, reaching for a star. her hands tease her wet box. she turns and moves ahead. to him she is reaching for desire. abdomen wavers as she slides. scarred fists to her breasts. hard, firm, nipples stabbing at silk-brown skin. she finds the star. in her, her hand touches the softness. the bed hard, she spreads her meal over the blanket. he stands. he breathes, he moans, stroking, stroking the flatness of the room. she is inside her world. she is safe.

BLITZZZZZZ

iN THE CORNER OF THE ROOM. THE BED'S BROWN EDGE FRAMES HER BODY. SHE LIES diagonally, underneath him. covers splayed, clumped, wrinkled. lay around the edges of the mattress. onto the floor. on the carpet their clothes, sleep. shadows run behind the closed door. back and forth, up down. woolly, dirty, carpet spirals. they love. he kisses her mouth, neck, shoulders. hands slither across curves, spaces, forms. shades cover the window. light creeps under. three jets. shadows of black stream between. lost in his body she hungers for him. her mouth moves over his shoul-

tensecondsofecstasy,

ders. across his chest. tongue flickers across hard, brown nipples. moans in the light. across the bed she reaches for water. everywhere is wet. a spoon sits, quietly on a table. She swings across him. feet landing, softly on air. he wraps his arms around her waist. kisses, licks, chews her soft, strong back. bony hands reach for a triangle. paper folded, like a hat. he grunts, peers over her shoulder. tongue licking, water. his breath quivers in her ear. anticipates her, as she sprinkles the white, into the quiet spoon. naked, they sit. touching, electric, petrified skins. she strokes his thigh. hair ignites, alert. she bends. he reaches between her legs, strokes. her target, on the floor. rigid, smooth, cylindrical. it lays, in shadow. calling beckoning, her. to come. touch me. lift. take her, shake her, carry her. far away. sick, with anticipation. she turns, to him. enraptures his mouth with hers. pulling hard, hair spread, legs, reaching. to the floor. she picks up the missile. dips it into water. he, moans. quivers, as she squirts. from the spike to the spoon. running fingers rip at her. mixing. tearing, to purify. absorbing essence. clenched jaws, fists. bound off, concurrent. little red spurt. nothing will hurt. rushhhhing, rushhhing, hummming, echoes. vision vortex. buses screeeam from the street. assaulting their, haaaaaaaaaven. loud whispers blitz through shrieking sense. numb, arms grab, rip, pull, grope. strobing screeching, breath. everywhere. shaking, shaking eyes. trembling hands legs. water, water. falling, to the bed. tensecondsofecstasy, together.

How To Fly

I STOOD AT THE CORNER. I WAS WAITING. IT SEEMED LIKE I WAS ALWAYS WAITING. for you, I guess. I watched, blurry-eyed, as cars passed by. The people in them happy, perhaps. They had been out, together. They went on dates, celebrating, partying. Where was I? When all these people were having fun. I just stood. I felt very stiff, or scared. I acted differently. I was different. Then I was there. In that moment. Yet no one knew, who or where I was. Far, far inside, I stood. Just waiting. A man passed by. He asked me for a date.

—Are you an officer of the law? I challenged.

—No.

—Let's take a walk.

I was wearing jeans and a tight black top. It had cooled somewhat over the morning. I felt, cool. I have always thought it odd that the skin eases the mind into its reality. It had been cooler now, for some time. We walked past the rows of two-storey buildings. Brown brick and glass and metal dissolved into brightly lit doorways. The light hurt my eyes.

—Hey babe, where you goin'? You comin' back? I know you lookin'. Come back, we'll groove.

I looked up from the pavement and saw a face in a doorway.

—Stay cool, I replied. I won't be long.

After a few more steps I told my date

—Hundred for a fuck, fifty a blow.

—That's too much.

—Of course it is, if you like getting shitty head. I'm special. You're in for a treat.

—Well I can get head up the street for thirty. How about thirty.

—What's the matter. You don' wanna fuck me or what? You'll catch the dose from those scags up there. Come on, let's go. I don't got all fuckin' night.

He reached out and touched my breast. It felt, good. I let him continue for a moment.

—They're nice aren't they? I said. They're yours for fifty, and of course I'll suck your cock so good you'll scream to fuck me baby.

—Forty bucks is all I've got. I like you, you're nice.

I looked around. It was getting colder, darker, quieter. It smelled like rain.

—All right let's go. Forty for head, and you can touch my tits. We walked into an alley I knew intimately. It was dark, dirty and the reek of mouldy garlic bread and stale red wine pierced the back of my throat. The light caught the edges of the alley. Up the middle it was shadowy, grey. He leaned up against a wall. The bricks framed his fat body. He tried to kiss me.

—No kissing.

I got on my knees, unzipped his fly. I remembered that I had been at a bar with my friends earlier. They had all gone home, together. It was late and I was unprepared to leave. I needed.

My father and I always drank together. I can't remember a time when he didn't offer me a drink from his bottle. I was so little and I smiled. I adored him. He was always doing something when he drank. I would just hang around him, waiting. His hands always seemed so gentle and strong. He would bend and offer me the bottle. I reached up anxiously, eagerly, slowly. It shone like the brightest star. His hands would help me tip it to my mouth. The fizz filled my nose and I laughed. I wanted more. I wanted it to go on forever. I stood waiting. Playing, in my mind. Games of Daddy and me. Happy, happy together. No one, nothing else around. Maybe a dog. Painting, baseball, riding on the tractor. I loved to ride on the tractor with my Dad. The two of us cruising slowly over the field. He helped me steer. I was small and rode in front of him. The grass would disappear underneath the dangerous part of the tractor. The part where I was never to put my hands. I could hear the birds chirping over the roaring of the motor. As far as my eyes would wander, I saw brown, green, yellow. Rough scratchy grass tempered by a powdery, pale, brilliant sky. We rode toward that sky, my Dad and I, so small. I cried for fear of ending it all, so sad, so sweet and us above all. The sun would dry my streaky face. With my Dad's soft hanky I blew my nose.

—Blow.

He offered his hand to my tear. I hugged him so hard and he patted my back.

—That's O.K. sweetheart. Don't cry, it's all right.

Back on the tractor and homeward we drive. He lets me steer, alone. I'm a big girl.

I stood up and looked across the alley. I had a rubbery taste in my mouth. I turned and walked in the shadow. In my pocket I felt the money. I looked at the black cracks beneath me, strewn with garbage. Remnants of people together and apart. Around the corner in the light, I saw a shape. My eyes slowly drew my head up.

—Yo sugar. You ready?

—Yeah, I whispered. Let's go.

I saw my feet stepping forward. I followed them.

—You gonna like this stuff. Maybe you gonna have to wait outside while I go in an' cop. Soon we be flyin'.

I saw the raindrops in some headlights.

Lydia Lunch
Cruel Story of Youth

H E WAS BORN ADDICTED TO HEROIN ON THE 19TH OF MARCH 1971 IN the L.A. County Community Hospital. Conceived in hate, abuse began in the womb. Another unwanted, unwelcome Latin loser born into the life cycle of a living hell. He came out screaming, contorted in pain. Twisted faces grimaced at the sight of another newborn junkie saddled with the sins of his forefathers. His papa left mama before the delivery hoping to score a dimebag in order to celebrate the fact that he wasn't born brain-dead or deformed, just a little bit fucked-up. Papa never returned after busting up his bike on the way back from East L.A. ... where the local cholos insisted he join them in a toast to his first and only newly begotten son. Jack and smack didn't mix too well and daddy took a spill which wiped the shit-eating grin clear off his puss. He never tried to see his son again. Mama didn't mind too much, blind to every need except the gnawing in her belly, the bruises between her skinny legs and the unscratchable bitch of her addiction. She took the next shot on the delivery table twelve minutes after the prodigal son was shat out like a watermelon.

His first meal was a weaning of morphine and methadone. A failed attempt to quell the spasms racking through his bloated little belly. He kicked and cried and tried to wish himself dead in the cradle of the nursery surrounded by other undeserving misfortunates. All victims of boozy blood fucks, lust and ritual gang bangs. None however less wanted than he was. None more tempered with a vengeance to destroy the lousy fuckers who condemned him to his life sentence under the rule of pain and hate. And never a more hate-filled fucker than he was destined to become.

Beautiful black (is the colour of my true love's) hair, smooth brown skin, (how I love) the son of the devil's advocate who grew up with a chip on his shoulder the size of the Boulder Dam. At the age of four he was beaten into his first coma by mommy's latest lover. Back in

L.A. County he remained for three weeks while they traced the swelling and clotting hoping that permanent damage wouldn't result from the contusion suffered from the blow from the big black man's left hand. That he lived was a shining testimonial to his predestined mission. A life-long tribunal littered with the scarring of the self-serving. At six he was witness to the degenerate urges of a third-generation coven of practising devil worshippers. Passed from mouth to cock to crack, his mother initiated him into the Church of Satan. One of many fuck toys brought into the delirious circle of the chronically demented, he was taught to please others and to enjoy the natural desires he was too young to deny himself. He quickly became an unquenchable suitor in the pursuits of his own pleasures. Like so many others born into the cleansing circle of fated pain, he learned first how to turn his hatred against himself. And then against everyone else. At the world-weary age of ten, he had already instigated an involvement with the next-door neighbours, a family of eleven, who took turns taking out their multiple frustrations on his battered hide. Mother, father, grandmother, daughters, suitors and sons, from six to sixty, beat at his bound and gagged body. Calling out the names of saints, sinners and each other, they prodded, poked and pronged themselves into his willing flesh. Like Christians at the altar of worship they whipped him into a ritual frenzy. Cursing in the name of Satan and salvation, they cleansed themselves of evil influence using him as a receptacle of their own perverted restitutions. Two years later the beatings stopped, although he claimed to never really tire of the abuse, he just needed stronger doses than what the granny's family could any longer deal out. He took his frustrations elsewhere and began his search for a suitable partner. At the age of twelve he moved in with three other delinquents, themselves no strangers to cruelty. Living in Hollywood, he began practising up on his charming ways, fine-honing his skills of verbal manipulation. The only rule in the house at 452 Franklin Avenue was that female flesh was to be tasted by all members of his new family ... THE WHORESOME FOURSOME as they soon became notorious. In rancid squalor the petty abuse of these four juvenile tyrants was unparalleled. Filthy Swedish magazines littered the hovel, inspiring them forward and on to new horrors. The wrecked room was home to the ritual degeneracy dished up to the unending string of teenage girls foolish enough to be coaxed over. Whips, wire and various hardware hung suspended from the ceiling and walls, the only order in an otherwise dishevelled bunker. The usual trick employed was to send the youngest and the prettiest, usually him, into the evening sunset with one goal in mind. Food for thought. Fodder for abuse. Once inside, the more-often-than-not intoxicated young bait was blindfolded, beaten and raped by whoever was present at the time. Taking turns on the tender flesh, cigarettes seared inner thighs, bottles broke on kneecaps and fingers, fists and bricks did what they did best. Batter. Bruise and bleed. Sex came as the final reward. Here the young lords lacerated every opening with a vengeful deliverance. Tortures employed were waylaid on the replicants who stood before them, reminiscent of the mothers they abhorred.

They, like their daddies before them, harboured the disease of a sexual affliction harnessed in by the reins of a superior physical dominance. After one particularly gruesome escapade involving the genital sacrifice of a fifteen-year-old girl from the valley, the police force was summoned, thus ending the two-year reign of terror in this unholy house of horrors. Since all participants were still underage, no charges could possibly be pressed, so the cops simply destroyed what remained inside the house, insisting on the immediate evacuation of 452 Franklin Avenue.

With no bridges left to burn, at the tender age of fourteen, he was forced to return to his mother. Strung out on dope, pills and alcohol, his insidious habits forced him into an even more grisly pattern of deviations. Sporting a one-hundred-and-twenty-five-dollar-a-day habit, his nocturnal predatorials led him into the alleys and backstreets of downtown L.A., where he began to prey upon smacked-out transvestites. Befriending a gaggle of the least homely Mexican and black queens, he began pimping and prostituting right alongside them. Nights would wind down around six a.m. with him gathered round the "girls" collecting his thirty per cent of the take. Demanding a recount of blow jobs, hand jobs and fist fucks administered, sympathizing generously with the most busted-up of the crew, he would take that wretch aside, insist upon a tear-soaked butt fuck, and after beating maliciously the whore about the head and neck would rifle through the pockets and purse, removing all but a ten-dollar bill. With a final kick up the ass, he'd send the queen falling onto his knees on the pavement and smirkily stride off in search of a score. Puking on the first rush of the day, he'd wipe the bile from his pant legs and lips and head back to crash on his mother's sofa.

In July '85 the walls came crashing in once more, when for the third time that year he had his nose busted with a vacuum-cleaner hose by his mother's latest lover, a would-be musician. In the heat of that sweltering mid-summer's night, with bandages still intact, he ran into his mother's bedroom and stabbed the bastard smack in the heart with a small stainless steel buck knife. Driving the blade deep inside the thick muscle, he cursed at the drunken bastard to get out … get the fuck out … leave me alone, leave my mother alone … I'll kill you … I swear to God I'll kill you … With fists bathed in blood, he pounded on the swelling gash attempting to right the wrongs heaped upon the household under the blithering barbarian's rule.

Self-defence landed him in juvenile detention until his sixteenth birthday. Once inside he learned the joys of self-mutilation, and how by hurting yourself more than anyone else would ever care to want to, he earned the respect of the other inmates. Always the first one to fight, the hammering blows which pounded into him while outnumbered three to one could never match the viciousness which he would later wreak upon himself. Alone in his bunk, the head-bashing would begin. Smashing his skull into the damp cement walls was the only way he knew to make the hurt go away. Replacing an indescribable pain somewhere in the base of his brain with a concentrated self-inflicted throbbing somehow made the burden of his hatred easier to deal with. It was the same with the broken glass and rusty knifetips. It brought relief waiting for scabs and bruises to slowly gently heal, knowing that they eventually would. Not as much could be said for the psychic or spiritual wounds left over from his life in holy hell.

He was released on his sixteenth birthday after a two-year incarceration. Custody was granted to his mother who by now couldn't stand the sight of him. Or the way his presence interfered with her endless stream of fuck-ups. She had a thing for alcoholic pill-poppers, castoffs from *Easy Rider, Dirty Harry, A Streetcar Named Desire*. Men who had done more than their fair share of stretches in Sing Sing, Camirillo and San Quentin. The kind of cunts who didn't give a fuck how hard their lives were as long as they could make someone else equally miserable. And that usually meant him.

He was out of juvenile only two weeks when mom's latest edition busted his face against the kitchen sink, breaking out three of his top front teeth. Blood splattered all over the white linoleum, and he was told to clean it up, pick up his teeth and take them over to the free clinic in East Hollywood. Laughing hysterically and sobbing between gales, he spat a big wad of blood and phlegm onto the left cheek of the Peter Fonda look-alike who punched him repeatedly in the face. But he stood tough, tear-stained blood drops running down his chin, laughing only when the fucker reached for the frying pan. He ran through the house swearing tearing out the front door, slamming it behind him. The cast iron skillet bolted out after him, crashing mightily into the centre of his forehead. Screaming at the top of his lungs for the wasted mongrel to come and prove what a big man he was, what kind of chicken-shit sissy low-life motherfucker fights with frying pans anyway. Fuck you man. And just as he's flipping the bastard off a '67 beat-to-shit Ford Fairlane comes barrelling around the corner his mother at the wheel knocking our young hero flat on his busted ass, where his head smashes into the fender and a concussion follows. His mother backs the car up, after nearly killing him in a jealous stupor of hostility and hate. After all, mama had to stand defensively beside her raving madman. I mean she knew a good thing when she had one and was hoping all these riled-up emotions would soon be employed in another glorious raging hate fuck. Wasn't that the only reason she had for tolerating these child-hating wife-beaters? The sexual delirium their mania would plunge her into … that freefall; the spiral.

He wakes up in L.A. County two days later with a note taped to the bedside table. Please don't come home is all it says. No love mom, no love nothing. He pulls the tube from his nose, rejects the I.V. hose from his right arm and gets dressed. A man with a mission. Dizzy and penniless he thumbs a ride the six and a half miles home, stopping first at the Ralph's Supermarket on La Brea Avenue. Determined not to get caught, he proudly saunters over to the hardware section, shoplifting three bottles of lighter fluid, a large box of matches and a Hershey's chocolate bar. He heads off down Sunset steely-eyed.

Sneaking around to the back of the house, he kicks open the basement window. Pummelling the glass with steel boot-tips. He finds his mother passed out on the living room couch, a dirty black slip hiked to the hips. Popping the safety lock on the first bottle of lighter fluid, he draws a heart around the witch, kissing her softly on the cheek, he whispers in her ear "there's no place like home, there's no place like home," he leaves a trail of thick spittle running down her chin. Slapping her once in the face, for good luck, she twitches and calls out Johnny, Johnny is that you … he lies and coos yeah, it's me … don't get up, I'm just going down to the liquor store … I'll be right back. She rolls over, a tiny smile crossing her twisted lips. He pulls one of her cigarettes from the full pack beside her and lights up. Blowing out the first match, he anoints her with the liquid combustible, baptizing her with the sign of the cross. Chanting in Latin he begins to pray … DREAD LORD OF THE DARK FLAME GIVE POWER … I DID NOT CONDEMN THEM. THEY CONDEMNED THEMSELVES. INFORMED OF THEIR INDISCRETIONS, I HAD NO CHOICE, WHEN CONFRONTED WITH THE EVIDENCE. THEY HAD BECOME ARROGANT IN THEIR MANNER TOWARDS THE GUARDIANS OF DECENCY, THEY CONDUCTED STRANGE DARK RITES, UNHOLY & TERRIBLE, WHICH VIOLATED THE PRECINCTS OF THE CHURCH. SO HE CONDEMNED THEM TO DEATH. IT WAS ONLY RIGHT. DREAD LORD OF THE DARK FLAME GIVE POWER. HAIL SATAN.

Kneeling beside her, he sets her thick black hair on fire. The damp couch quickly ignites, the circle of fire engulfing her sleepy body. A ring of fire in the shape of a horseshoe burns brightly, quietly. Backing up out of the heat, he traces her name in butane on the tables and chairs. Rifling through her purse, he stuffs his pockets with dollars and change. Emptying the leftovers of the two canisters, he watches the lighter fluid burn a beautiful soothing blue. He backs out the front door, savouring the miracle of the flames, unable to pull himself away from such a delicious spectacle. His reverie overpowers. Stuck in place, a massive erection swells from his gut. With half-closed eyes, he begins groping, fondling, pulling on himself. The heat and smell of burning hair stimulating unknown pleasures. Jacking roughly ready to spout, he drops to his knees swearing Spanish. Cursing his mother with Satanic litanies recollected from his tortured childhood. WHAT MEN ARE THEY WHO HAUNT THESE FATAL GLOOMS, & FILL THEIR LIVING MOUTHS WITH DUST OF DEATH, & MAKE THEIR HABITATIONS IN THE TOMBS, & BREATHE ETERNAL SIGHS WITH MORTAL BREATH, & PIERCE LIFE'S VEIL OF VARIOUS ERROR, TO REACH THAT VOID OF DARKNESS & OLD TERROR. THE VILEST THING MUST BE LESS VILE THAN THOU, FROM WHOM IT HAD ITS BEING, GOD & LORD, CREATOR OF ALL WOE & SIN, ABHORRED, MALIGNANT & IMPLACABLE. I VOW THAT NOT FOR ALL THY POWER FURLED & UNFURLED, FOR ALL THE TEMPLES TO THY GLORY BUILT, WOULD I ASSUME THE IGNOMINIOUS GUILT OF HAVING MADE SUCH MEN IN SUCH A WORLD. DESECRATION. HE SPEWED FORTH A VILE, RANK & CANTANKEROUS SPEW WHICH SHOT HALFWAY ACROSS THE ROOM A DROPLET LANDING ON MOMMY'S LIPS. EXHAUSTED & NEARLY DELIRIOUS HE BROKE OUT IN A

FIT OF LAUGHTER. ROLLING AROUND IN CIRCLES ON THE FLOOR, THE FLAMES LICKED AT A LOCK OF HIS OWN HAIR. BEATING HIMSELF ABOUT THE HEAD, HE EXTINGUISHED THE SMALL BLAZE & DECIDED TO GET THE FUCK OUT.

ONCE OUTSIDE THE SWELTERING INFERNO HE FELT RELIEVED. FREE OF SIN, OF GUILT, OF SHAME. RELEASED, SET FREE. STOPPING TO COUNT THE CASH COLLECTED FROM THE DYING WOMAN'S BAG, HE GATHERED HIS BREATH. IT WAS AT THIS VERY UNFORTUNATE INTERVAL THAT HIS GRANDFATHER, THE RETIRED WORLD WAR II DRILL SERGEANT, DECIDES TO PULL UP. SPRINTING OUT OF THE CAR, MANIACAL GRIN EAR TO EAR, GRANDPA BARRELS IN FOR A BONECRUSHING BEARHUG, LIFTING HIM CLEAR OFF THE GROUND, SPINNING HIM IN CENTRIFUGAL CIRCLES. "HOW THE HELL ARE YOU … LONG TIME NO SEE …" "YEAH, FOUR OR FIVE YEARS," THE WISE ONE REPLIES … "SO YOU'RE OUT …" "YEAH, I'M OUT …" "WELL LET'S GO INSIDE …" "NO … MY MOTHER'S SLEEPING …" "AT THIS HOUR OF THE DAY???" AND WITH NO CHOICE LEFT, HE'S DRAGGED TO THE FRONT DOOR, LOCKED IN A STURDY EMBRACE. AS THE OLD MAN GOES TO OPEN THE DOOR, HIS FINGERS SINGE ON THE HEAT OF THE METAL KNOB. TERRIFIED RECOGNITION CROSSES THE OLD MAN'S WAR-TORN FACE. TURNING SO THEY FACE EACH OTHER, HE BEGINS POUNDING FISTS & FEET AGAINST THE YOUNG PYRO'S PLIANT BODY. DEFENCELESS AGAINST THE BLOWS, HE ACCEPTS THEM WITH RESIGNATION. THIS WASN'T HIS FIRST ADVENTURE IN PUNISHMENT RENDERED FOR CRIMES COMMIT-TED. DRAGGING HIM ACROSS THE LAWN TO THE NEAREST NEIGHBOURS, HELD IN A VISE-LIKE HEADLOCK, THERE WAS NO CHANCE FOR ESCAPE. HE DIDN'T EVEN FUCKING BOTHER.

THE AMBULANCE WAS THE FIRST TO ARRIVE, FOLLOWED QUICKLY BY THE POLICE & FIRE DEPARTMENT. HE WAS ROUGHLY HANDCUFFED, SHOVED IN THE BACK OF THE POLICE VAN & RETURNED ONCE MORE TO "JUVIE," WHERE HE WAS TO SPEND SIX MORE MISERABLE MONTHS, UNTIL ON HIS EIGHTEENTH BIRTHDAY HE WAS RELEASED ON GOOD BEHAVIOUR.

HE GOT OUT TO GET STRUNG-OUT AGAIN. THE PRESSURE AND LONE-LINESS WERE JUST TOO MUCH. NOWHERE TO GO NO ONE TO TALK TO. NO MONEY. NO DRUGS. NO NOTHING. HE STARTED HANGING OUT AT THE SLEAZY BARS ON HOLLYWOOD & VINE, PICKING UP ON AGEING GO-GO GIRLS, EX-STRIPPERS & PROSTITUTES. WOMEN USED TO HIS KIND OF ABUSE, WHO THROUGH SOME KIND OF DEFENCE MECHANISM

MISTOOK THIS TYPE OF ATTENTION FOR AFFECTION. ALL VICTIMS THEM-
SELVES OF LONELY LIVES LOST TO THE THIEVING STREETS. HE'D HOOK
THEM ON HIS OWN ADDICTION TO BONECRUSHING POWER FUCKS,
TWISTING THEM UP INSIDE UNTIL THEY'D LOVE HIM JUST ENOUGH TO
SUPPORT HIS VARIOUS BAD HABITS. DUST, SPEED, COKE AND DOPE COCK-
TAILS SPURRED ON HIS NEED FOR RETRIBUTION. USING ANY AVAILABLE
ICON, HE PUNISHED FEROCIOUSLY THE SINS OF HIS MOTHER. BANGING
HIS FULL BODY WEIGHT INTO THE WILLING RECEPTORS, EVERY SEXUAL
ESCAPADE BECAME AN ACT OF UNMITIGATED VIOLENCE. AS BLOOD RACED
FROM BRAIN CELLS, FISTS BECAME ENGORGED. OUTRAGED. POUNDING
INSIDE THEM, PUNCHING WOULD FOLLOW. BLACK EYES, BRUISED LIPS,
BLOOD CLOTS, TEARDROPS. HE TOOK OUT ON THEM WHAT THE REST
OF HIS WORLD TOOK OUT ON HIM. EIGHTEEN YEARS OF HARDSHIP,
MISHAP AND HELLFIRE WOULD BOIL OVER, BURSTING FORTH IN UNSTOP-
PABLE RITES, SPASMS. HIS ONLY SATISFACTION CAME THROUGH
ANOTHER'S ANNIHILATION. TO MAKE THEM HURT AS MUCH AS HE DID
WAS THE ONLY WAY TO RELIEVE THE PAIN HE COULD NO LONGER
BEAR RELIVING.

It was a late autumn night after a serious session of titty torture and humiliation involving Patty, a burnt-out thirty-three-year-old ex-Vegas showgirl fallen on hard times and bad
luck, that he stumbled upon his near mirror reflection. A beautiful young Latino girl was
sprawled in the alley in back of the showgirl's crash pad. Thinking her just drunk and fucked-
up he stumbled over kicking the teenager in the ribs. Hard. No reply. He kicked her twice
in the ass, nothing. He cracked her head against the dumpster. No response. He slapped her
soft velvety face. Dead. O.D.'d. Dosed. Crumpled into a small, wet, raggedy heap. Littered
before him. He bent down, stuck his hands in her pockets. Thirty bucks and an out-of-town
I.D. stating she was fifteen. He took the needle from her inner elbow, tasting the blood-
encrusted junk. Not bad, he mumbled, lifting the tiny girl up, over his shoulder, slipping
her quietly into the trash receptacle. Looking back to make sure no one had seen, he travelled east, hoping to score a quick dime. Within minutes he was fixing two alleyways away,
using the very same needle recovered from the human wreckage left rotting in the garbage
can. No sooner had the shit started rocketing into his bloodstream than the bile pushed forward pulsing into his throat, out his mouth. Not bad, he grumbled, stoned but still bitter.
He sank to his knees, tumbling forward. The weight of his heartless disconcern crashing in
on him. The realization that he had become everything he had hated in everybody else was
a burden he was not prepared to face. He picked up the dejected works, plunging the spike
over and over into his arms, wrists, hands, neck. Stabbing wildly he was searching frantically
for a valve that would unhinge, release, set free. Trying to find a black hole somewhere inside
that once plundered would concentrate all the pain and horror and heartache into a solid-
bodied centre. Looking for a way into the void that would lovingly engulf, embrace,

surround, erase. Looking for somewhere, somehow, someone who could help him to house the unending cycle of pain and hate. Looking for someone like me.

THE END

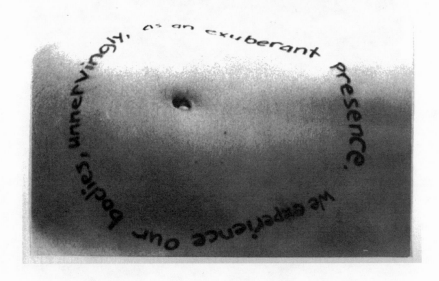

"This is impenetrable anatomy ..."

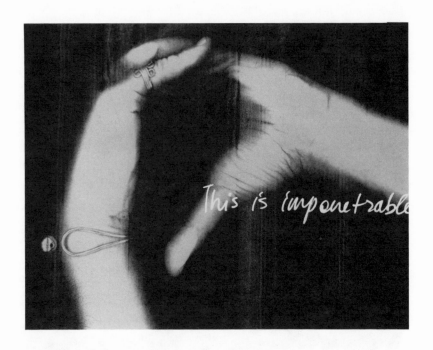

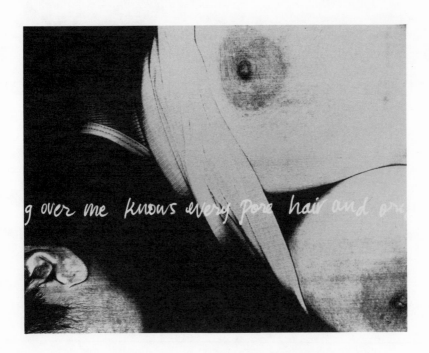

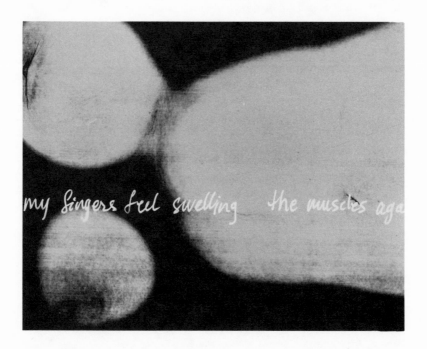

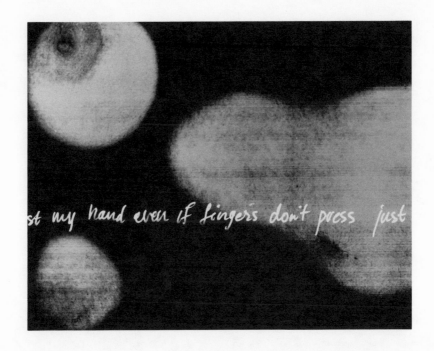

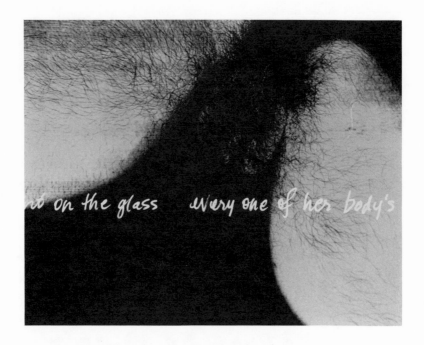

Erica Jong
Fruits & Vegetables

apples

1

Goodbye, he waved, entering the apple.
That red siren,
whose white flesh turns brown
with prolonged exposure to air,
opened her perfect cheeks to receive him.
She took him in.
The garden revolved
in her glossy patinas of skin.
Goodbye.

2
O note the two round holes in onion. *onion*

3
Did I tell you about
my mother's avocado?
She grew it from a pit.
Secretly, slowly in the dark,
it put out grub-white roots
which filled a jelly jar.
From this unlikely start,
an avocado tree with bark
& dark green leaves

avocado

shaded the green silk couch
which shaded me
throughout my shady adolescence.
There, beneath that tree
my skirt gave birth to hands!
Oh memorable hands of boys
with blacked-out eyes
like culprits
in the *National Enquirer.*
My mother nursed that tree
like all her children,
turned it around so often
towards the sun
that its trunk grew twisted
as an old riverbed,
& despite its gaudy leaves
it never bore
fruit.

4

Cantaloupes: the setting sun at Paestum
slashed by rosy columns.

5

cantaloupes

I am thinking of the onion again, with its two O mouths, like the gaping holes in nobody.
Of the outer skin, pinkish brown, peeled to reveal a greenish sphere, bald as a dead planet,
glib as glass, & an odour almost animal. I consider its ability to draw tears, its capacity
for self-scrutiny, flaying itself away, layer on layer, in search of its heart which is simply
another region of skin, but deeper & greener. I remember Peer Gynt. I consider its sometimes double heart. Then I think of despair when the onion searches its soul & finds only
its various skins; & I think of the dried tuft of roots leading nowhere & the parched
umbilicus, lopped off in the garden. Not self-righteous like the proletarian potato, nor a
siren like the apple. No show-off like the banana. But a modest, self-effacing vegetable,
questioning, introspective, peeling itself away, or merely radiating halos like lake ripples.
I consider it the eternal outsider, the middle child, the sad analysand of the vegetable kingdom. Glorified only in France (otherwise silent sustainer of soups & stews), unloved for
itself alone—no wonder it draws our tears! Then I think again how the outer peel resem-
bles paper, how soul & skin merge into one, how each peeling strips bare a heart which
in turn turns skin …

bananas

6

A poet in a world without onions,
in a world without apples
regards the earth as a great fruit.

Far off, galaxies glitter like currants.
The whole edible universe drops
currants   to his watering mouth …

Think of generations of mystics
salivating for the fruit of god,
of poets yearning to inhabit apples,
of the sea, that dark fruit,
closing much more quickly than a wound,
of the nameless galaxies of astronomers,
hoping that the cosmos will ripen
& their eyes will become tongues …

7

For the taste of the fruit
is the tongue's dream,
& the apple's red
is the passion of the eye.

8

If a woman wants to be a poet,
she must dwell in the house of the tomato.

t o m a t

9

It is not an emptiness,
the fruit between your legs,
but the long hall of history,
& dreams are coming down the hall
by moonlight.

10

They push up through the loam
like lips of mushrooms.

11

(Artichoke, after Child): Holding the heart base up, rotate it slowly with your left hand against the blade of a knife held firmly in your right hand to remove all pieces of ambition & expose the pale surface of the heart. Frequently rub the cut portions with gall. Drop each heart as it is finished into acidulated water. The choke can be removed after cooking.

12

(Artichoke, after Neruda)

It is green at the artichoke heart,
but remember the times
you flayed
leaf after leaf,
hoarding the pale silver paste
behind the fortresses of your teeth,
tonguing the vinaigrette,
only to find the husk of a worm
at the artichoke heart?
The palate reels like a wronged lover.
Was all that sweetness counterfeit?
Must you vomit back
world after vegetable world
for the sake of one worm
in the green garden of the heart?

artichoke

heart

13

But the poem about bananas has not yet been written. Southerners worry a lot about bananas. Their skin. And nearly everyone worries about the size of bananas, as if that had anything to do with flavour. Small bananas are sometimes quite sweet. But bananas are like poets: they only want to be told how great they are. Green bananas want to be told they're ripe. According to Freud, girls envy bananas. In America, chocolate syrup & whipped cream have been known to enhance the flavour of bananas. This is called a *banana split*.

14

The rice is pregnant.
It swells past its old transparency.
Hard, translucent worlds inside the grains
open like fans. It is raining rice!
The peasants stand under oiled
rice paper umbrellas cheering.

Someone is scattering rice from the sky!
Chopper blades mash the clouds.
The sky browns like cheese soufflé.
Rice grains puff & pop open.

"What have we done to deserve this?"
the peasants cry. Even the babies
are cheering. Cheers slide from their lips
like spittle. Old men kick their clogs
into the air & run in the rice paddies
barefoot. This is a monsoon! A wedding!

Each grain has a tiny invisible parachute.
Each grain is a rain drop.

"They have sent us rice!" the mothers scream,
opening their throats to the smoke ...

15

Here should be a picture of my favourite apple.
It is also a nude & bottle.
It is also a landscape.
There are no such things as still lives.

16

In general, modern poetry requires (underline one): a) more fruit; b) less fruit; c) more
vegetables; d) less vegetables; e) all of the above; f) none of the above.

17

Astonishment of apples. Every fall.
But only Italians are into grapes,
calling them *eggs*.
O my eggs,
branching off my family tree,
my father used to pluck you,
leaving bare twigs on the dining room table,
leaving mother furious on the dining room table:
picked clean.
Bare ruined choirs
where late the sweet.
A pile of pits.

e g g s

18

Adam naming the fruit
after the creation of fruit,
his tongue tickling
the crimson lips of the pomegranate,
the tip of his penis licking
the cheeks of the peach,
quince petals in his hair,
his blue arms full of plums,
his legs wrapped around watermelons,
dandling pumpkins on his fatherly knees,
tomatoes heaped around him in red pyramids . .

watermelons

     peach
     peach
     peach
     peach
     peach

        he sighs

to kingdom come.

The Long Tunnel of Wanting You

This is the long tunnel of wanting you.
Its walls are lined with remembered kisses
wet & red as the inside of your mouth,
full & juicy as your probing tongue,
warm as your belly against mine,
deep as your navel leading home,
soft as your sleeping cock beginning to stir,
tight as your legs wrapped around mine,
straight as your toes pointing toward the bed
as you roll over & thrust your hardness
into the long tunnel of my wanting,
seeding it with dreams & unbearable hope,
making memories of the future,

making memories of the future,
straightening out my crooked past,
teaching me to live in the present present tense
with the past perfect and the uncertain future
suddenly certain for certain
in the long tunnel of my old wanting
which before always had an ending
but now begins & begins again
with you, with you, with you.

Love Magick

Oh for a candle I could light
to draw you closer ...
Oh for a poppet
made like you,
with your own lovely body
sewn again of cloth,
with your own pale
unseeing eyes,
with your own cock sweetly curving,
remade in wax or clay ....

Oh for an herb
to place upon my tongue
to bring your tongue
to mine ....

Oh for a potion
I could drink
or slip to you
at some stale
dinner party ....

Oh for your nail parings ...
Oh for your hairs ...
stirred in a brew,
baked in a millet cake ....

I would make a stew,
a soup, a witch's mix
to bring your lovely thighs
on mine.

I would boil bats if not babies
& toads if not theologians
to make you care ....

I would enter your blood
like malaria, enter your eyes
like laser beams, enter your palms
like the holy spirit
causing stigmata
to a sex-starved saint!

Oh love,
I would spell you
evol
if mere anagrams
would bring you
near ....

But I spell you *love*
& still
you do not
hear.

Mary Louise Adams

Episode 1

Citric Encounter

SHE WANTS SEX WITH THE PUNGENCY OF A FRESHLY SLICED LIME, WITH THE fervid intensity of a sweltering summer afternoon. I want her to be happy, to feel the briny pleasure of a gleaming cunt.

I go to see her.

I arrive in good time. We chat. I remark on her hair, the way the light plays a bronze and copper medley as it falls across her back. She smiles appropriately at the compliment. I look around her room, at the books, the clothes. I take my time. I'm comfortable. I can feel her watching me. I like that. I like the pressure of her look on my back. We are both silent. Outside, the wind tests the give in an ancient branch.

Each of several minutes leaves us behind until her cinnamon smell cuts at my nonchalance and I turn to her. She meets my eyes with a compelling gaze and my hands, wrists, elbows slide around her waist and we kiss. Anxious tongues between relenting lips, bellies pressed flat, breast nestled beside breast. Abruptly she removes my clothes, pulls me to her and we kiss again. The wool of her trousers chafes my skin while the bones of her hips trace a steady path along my pelvis, back and forth and up and around, I graciously take her lead, back and forth and up and around until tenderly, persuasively, she pulls me to the wall and like a rag doll shadow I follow to find my spine against cool plaster and her fine solid body supporting me, pinning my hands while she laps and sucks at my shoulders and breasts with an aggressive supple tongue, at my torso, my groin. And her clothes come off and my hips arch to meet her and she drops to the floor to nuzzle the salt of my cunt and I have to hold myself steady against the touch of her tongue but my legs give and I slip to my knees I slip to my ass I slip to my back and then she's down on me, her own cunt wet on my mouth cheeks chin. Our skins fairly glisten.

If I just ease up my hand it's pillowed between slick swollen lips. I leave it there. Her breath catches, the caressing tongue rests. And I fuck her. Willing, straining muscles draw on my hand, pull against its skin. I move to pull back but she holds me there. I feel her breath heavy on my thigh and I push in past my knuckles to the cleft of my wrist and I've moved her to the floor and I'm holding her as she gets fucked as her hand grips my own and we rock and she's dripping and moaning and dripping and her warm salty smell's on my arms and legs, on the floor and we know this is good and we laugh and I'm out of her, on her, dropping wet greedy lusty kisses and the lime juice girl is emblazoned.

Aren't we clever? We knew just what to do.

Episode 2

So, I'm at the dance, dancing with a woman who is not you, thinking about you dancing with me. I try to focus on the woman at hand, but the song ends and she leaves abruptly. I stay and dance alone, giving in to my fantasy of dancing with you, fast and close, our breasts touching, our thighs pressed tightly together. With my eyes closed I imagine the weight of your hands on my back, your breath warm on my neck as you whisper into my ear. But again the music stops and I'm alone.

I leave the dance floor quickly. Through a maze of glowing cigarette butts and half-empty beer bottles I make my way outside. The cool evening air does nothing to settle my pulse; the image of us together remains on my mind.

I know you are alone. I run the blocks to your house and arrive at your door flushed, sweating and out of breath. Your light is on.

My key turns quietly in the lock and I startle you by letting myself in. You sit writing at your desk. In a plain white shirt and jeans you look more than a little butch.

"I've been thinking about you," you say as you drop your pen to come stand before me.

I'm still struggling to catch my breath, "What were you thinking?"

"Well," you take my hand and kiss each fingertip carefully, "I wanted you to be here. I wanted to turn you on." You start removing my clothes. "I wanted to make you crazy with wanting me to want you." You pause to study my now-bare torso. "I wanted to make you delirious with desire."

I laugh at your hyperbole, "You've high hopes," though it suits me fine to let you have your way.

My disrobing complete, you run your hand quickly over my nipples—just once—before making me kneel across a pillow on your big blue bed. I watch you deliberately choose two long scarves from a peg on the back of your door. I hold my breath, anticipating.

"I knew I'd get to do this one day," you say as you crawl behind me, letting the scarves drape loosely over my inner thighs. For the briefest moment I feel your hand on my ass but then it's gone and you've bound my ankles with silk. You tie my wrists behind my back before knotting the two pieces of fabric together. You're pleased with your handiwork and sit quietly for a long time, smiling like a cat.

It's with a calculated patience that you carry on with your seduction. Unbuckling your belt you pull it from your jeans and place it on my lap. Then button by button you open your fly and run your fingertips through the exposed dark hair. Though I can't see, I know you are playing with your clit. I imagine you touching me in the same way. You moan softly.

Unable to touch you, I want at least to see your cunt, your breasts. I want to smell you. But you refuse to rush. You proceed to roll your sleeves to your own exacting specifications. When you complete your task and look up, I note the flush of your cheeks, the deep red of your lips.

Finally you climb out of your jeans and I can see how wet you are, glistening and dripping on the blue cotton sheet beneath you. I lean closer but you push me back. A moan slips out from deep in my throat. I want to feel the wet of you on my hand, in my mouth. But it's your own hand that runs up and down your lips, slipping inside, straying back to your ass, brushing your clit. My hips move in response. I bend over wanting to rub my nipples against my thigh but you see and your hand goes still. Your gaze says watch and I do.

As one hand plays with your cunt the other, ever so carefully, unbuttons your shirt. Your nipples are hard and my tongue parts my lips, wanting that feeling between my teeth. You tease them, pinching them harder as you rub your clit. Your breath grows harsh and your skin reddens. My own body tenses as you come. For the next few moments you're still, watching me.

The waiting becomes too much. I ask you to touch me and you do—slowly and gently. The soft caresses infuriate me. "Harder." The word escapes through dry lips. You smile.

Your fingers curl around my nipples to pull and pinch, bringing them to lips that suck before giving way to teeth and tongue. Your hands are free to knead my back and my ass. My neglected cunt tries to push against you, but you ignore it, teasing my thighs with your belt. You kiss me hard, pressing your soft, full mouth on mine, forcing your teeth against my lips. I try to pull away for air but you kiss me again and again until our mouths are tender and I can see the red of your own lips deepen.

While I watch you watching me I feel your fingers brushing my cunt. You lay me on my side, reach for gloves and the jelly and then there are fingers in my ass and in my cunt and my nipples are in your mouth and I'm crying and pulling on the scarves and you fuck me harder and I'm pushing down on your fist and my cunt's everything and you're the warm, deep darkness that surrounds it and I'm not here any more.

You fuck me until my body grows still, until the wanting subsides. You untie the scarves slowly. We're covered in sweat and smells and salt. They hold us together as we fall asleep.

Patricia Seaman
The Dress

I'M CONVENIENTLY OUT. I'M CONVENIENTLY BUSY FOR TWO OR THREE WEEKS. sometimes I can't be bothered to answer the phone. Or else, I've unplugged the damn thing. Anyway, you haven't called. Did you call? I was out. Fortunately, you're very busy. The demands on your time, who would have believed it? Besides, you forgot about me in a week anyway. Thank you.

It was the dress that gave me so much pleasure. Just the dress. For one thing, it nearly fits me. Off the rack nothing does. I suppose it's a "sexy" dress. But that has nothing to do with me. Now I own a sexy dress, that's all. I couldn't be bothered to buy one before. I had no place to wear it. Now I wear it anywhere, all over the place. At the most surprising times, and it's not more inappropriate than anything else. So what?

It wasn't you ripping the dress, it was the sound of the dress ripping, if you get what I mean. Later you said that you heard the dress ripping. And you hardly knew me. There you were ripping my dress. While pleading silently with it to have some compassion. Begging it not to rip, unable not to rip it. The sound of the dress ripping.

You couldn't believe it because I didn't bat an eye. That's what you said, I didn't bat an eye.

And wearing it home, hiding it under my full-length overcoat. And a look of vagueness, a little defiant, walking, without fear, past three drunk men on a deserted street in the early hours of the morning.

I took some care with it. Using thin thread and my embroidery scissors, I repaired the damage. I had it cleaned and pressed.

I get so much pleasure from that dress.

I wore it to dinner at my sister's house. My little niece was nearly stupefied by the neckline. She is already waiting for one just like it. She is already waiting for the ten years to pass, keeping in mind the dress.

I, Mary

Makeda Silvera
The Girl Who Loved Weddings

I'M A GIRL WHO LOVES WEDDINGS. I REALLY DO. I'VE BEEN A BRIDESMAID TOO MANY times to count. Weddings can be so beautifully perfect. So romantic. Mystical even. The bride. Face full of hope. I've seen that look on women who'd lived with men many months or even years before the wedding. Women who already had children.

And still that look of wonder. That simple-hearted innocence, if only for those few cherished hours. I just love it. I can't help it. I don't know what it is. Yes, I do know, weddings just let you forget the ugliness of life.

The groom. Oh Lord, the groom. Protector. Provider. Till death do us part. Yeah, I can still hear those countless ministers. I love it, I tell you. I think weddings are one of the greatest theatrical performances on earth. Only the Bible is better scripted. I really mean it. And the faces of the guests, worth a million, those faces.

The hours tap away and the celebrations come to a close. The wedding stops and the marriage begins. For some, it's a hairpin curve in the road, for others it's just learning the traffic rules. Many, many years ago, I was asked to be a bridesmaid at my cousin Helena's wedding. It was to be a small occasion, and I the only bridesmaid. Without hesitation, I said yes.

She chose a small Anglican church for the wedding, close to their apartment, in fact right across from the funeral parlour where our grandfather was buried. Okay, he wasn't buried there. You know what I mean. Anyway, my cousin and I were pall-bearers at the funeral. You see, we come from a family with more than its share of women. When my cousin first told me about the wedding, I thought she was pregnant and, not to lose face, was getting married.

"Are you pregnant?" I asked her a few days before the ceremony. She threw her quick, nervous laugh in my face and answered back, "Don't be ridiculous. Nothing of the kind. I just don't want to live with him like this any more. Is that O.K.?" She had known him for three months, two of which they shacked up together.

My cousin was a girl with many curves, a pretty face, long straightened black hair that rested on her shoulders, and a smile so dazzling that it just about pulled you into her mouth.

Helena was an unpredictable girl. Not so long before she announced her wedding plans, she confided in me that she would never ever get married.

"Jenny," she said. "Girl, I know I will definitely not do this married thing, I don't want anyone controlling me. No way. I'm happy the way I am. I love them, but not enough to marry."

Of course, when we were both twelve years old, she'd said she would never have sex with a boy. In fact, if you want to know the truth, we had made that pledge to each other. But, no sooner said, she ran off with Everet Johnson when she was thirteen years old. Needless to say, cousin Helena fell in love several times after Everet Johnson. At fifteen, she wanted to be an actress, ran off to Calgary, then Vancouver and finally Quebec. She worked the bars as a striptease dancer and made some extra money on the side as an occasional small-time call girl.

One day I received an ominous brown package in the mail. It was from her. A full-page profile of Helena in a magazine called *Le Nouveau.*

Having never been to Montreal, I was not familiar with this magazine. I did recognize the full-page, colour nude centrefold though. There she was with her beautiful self, head high, black hair on brown shoulders and that award-winning smile. Her youthful naked body on view for the small price of a magazine. With my limited French, I set my sights on making sense out of the article.

Cousin Helena had changed her name to Natasha the stripper. In the interview, she said she was twenty-two years old. I looked into her then sixteen-year-old face, heavy with make-up, and wondered how on earth the interviewer could not see the youth in her. Did they even care? I wondered. Still, I could not help but chuckle at the parts of the interview I could understand. She claimed she had recently arrived in Quebec from the Caribbean. That cousin of mine. We were both Canadian-born of Caribbean parents, and we had only visited our parents' birthplace once. The more I read, the louder my laughter. She told the interviewer that she could never get used to the harsh Canadian winter, but the Canadian people were gentle and warm, less racist she said than across the border. What a sweet liar this cousin of mine.

I was at first embarrassed by the nude photo. Legs wide apart, one hand holding dark brown breast, the other bashfully covering her pubic hair. But I had to admit, she did look damn good. I quickly hid the newspaper away from my parents' inquisitive eyes.

When she got tired of Quebec, she ran off to Las Vegas, with a customer from a night-club she worked.

She returned home a year later, with a broken heart and a series of vaginal infections. But not for long, soon she was laughing her nervy laugh and chalking it all up to experience.

Some of our friends said she was crazy. "A loose screw somewhere," they used to say. But we paid no attention to their cruel talk. They're all just envious, I comforted her.

To me, Helena was just a free spirit. She courted adventure and lived life to its fullest. She was not content to live through books. I'm not saying that sometimes she didn't do crazy things, but not the craziness that sends you to the asylum. Goddammit, I would have been right beside her, and I'm not mad.

My cousin just had high spirits. Like the time she drove her father's car all the way to Niagara Falls without a licence. I was sitting deep in the back seat with Douglas, my first boyfriend. She with Everet Johnson. In fact it was a sweet ride and we didn't get caught. Does she sound like a candidate for a mental asylum? Oh yes, she did piss once in the middle of a department store to protest the treatment of a young immigrant boy caught shoplifting. Fortunately for us, we were not discovered.

Then there was the time we sneaked out my bedroom window on the second floor of our house to attend a dance. We were grounded, so asking permission was strictly out of the question. Desperate, we had to show our face at that school dance. Salvation came to us in the form of an eight-foot ladder, which we had hidden inconspicuously in my bedroom.

I was surprised we did not wake my parents when we came home. Our voices heavy with wine and our balance in question, we climbed into bed, where sleep soon found us, legs flung over legs.

There were many such adventures with cousin Helena. Then I broke the spell. Got married and separated shortly after. Helena continued to blaze ahead. Finally, she met Monty. Fell in love. Shacked up. Joined his church. And now they were to be married.

Monty was tall and slim. Quiet. A bit on the serious side. He didn't laugh easily. He was almost thirty years old, ten years older than Helena. Eight years my senior.

He wasn't ugly, but neither was he handsome. Monty's hair was shoulder length, like Helena's. Unlike Helena's straightened hair, he wore his in thick brown dreads. His eyes were a dark broody brown, coloured with red specks. He had a wide nose and full lips. His face sported a long thin cut on the right side, from his ears to the tip of his mouth. A knife-wound I learned later. A souvenir from his former days as a small-time hustler.

Monty was a guy with no trade. When he could, he worked as a packer in a meat market, but he never stayed long enough to get any seniority. Other times, he drove cabs.

The evenings I spent over at my cousin Helena's house he was easy enough to be around, though a bit unravelled in his thread of conversation.

He was an orthodox Rastafarian, though he did not attend church regularly. Many times I tried to engage him in discussions about his religion and the teachings of the movement, but to no avail. I was not ignorant of the Rastafarian philosophy and wanted to have a more in-depth discussion with Monty; but we never got past Ethiopia, Haile Selassie or the cloud of smoke always coming from his nostrils.

When I told Helena about his unwillingness to discuss his faith, Helena told me he was a deep thinker. To me Monty was a fraud. An incorrigible one. But the more I got to know him, the easier it was for me to understand my cousin's attraction to this man.

Once, furious after yet another demonstration to protest the injustice of the world, I stopped by their apartment. I was particulary agitated that day. My feet were swollen to almost twice their size. My clothes sticky and smelly from the hot sun and close crowd, the sounds of sirens and police force still in my ears. My cousin was not in. I was almost in tears as I threw myself onto the couch.

"When will this madness in South Africa end. When will Blacks have basic equal rights. Justice. Determination of their lives. I'm tired of pounding those damn pavements."

If he were a stranger in a crowded room, I would have gotten a better response. He was sitting right there next to me on the couch, nodding in agreement.

"Don't you have anything to say?" I asked, my voice quivering. "Where do you think this is all going to end? What do you think of people taking up arms, fighting violence with violence?" He must have been surprised by the tremor in my voice, for he responded somewhat.

"Well, whatever is necessary, though I is a peaceful man."

"Well, then," I pressed "what's to be done?"

"Well, Africa must be free no matter what." I looked at him, puzzled and disappointed with his answer. I opened my mouth to proceed, but he wandered off towards the bathroom with a match and a cigarette.

"I'm going to take a shit, help yourself to some food on the stove."

Deep thinker my ass. How could my cousin marry this jerk? At that moment if it weren't for my love for Helena and being a bridesmaid once again, I would have left that blasted apartment.

He was a long time on the toilet. When he finally emerged, he patted me on my shoulders and spoke like one who had just had a vision, "Don't get so worked up, little sister, leave everything to Jah. South Africa time soon come, and all dem wicked ones will get burn ..."

I was irritated but kept my comment to a heavy sigh.

"Let me play something to calm you down," he offered, walking over to the sound system. Curled up on the couch, I fell into a light sleep, listening to a selection of reggae singers and sniffing an occasional whiff of Monty's spliff. Music and joint: that was Mr. Deep Thinking future-cousin-in-law's answer to everything.

Despite Monty, I was still excited about the wedding. I myself had married young. Only eighteen years old. My husband ran out on me three months and four days after the ceremony. I know just when he left and why. We both found out I was barren. But my lack of menstrual blood did not bother me until my husband left me for a woman with a womb as big as a continent. In no time she gave him twins. I felt like hell on wheels. I was tormented by his happy family and ashamed that he'd walked out on me. Our ill-fated marriage was the talk of the town for a long time. I wanted to kill myself and I wanted revenge on him.

Ours was an old-fashioned Christian wedding. Two hundred guests on each side. I wore my mother's long white wedding gown. I'd even converted to Catholicism for him. In the overcrowded church, I repeated "Till death do us part."

For months after the marriage ended, I imagined ways of killing myself. Dreamed about the look of horror on his face, his guilt. I wasn't thinking feminism back then. I was possessed. I wanted only one thing. My man back. My marriage back. I wanted to marry all over again. I wanted to repeat those vows.

I took an overdose, a mixture of sleeping pills and aspirin, and woke up in the psychiatric ward. I resigned myself to a three-week involuntary stay. Another time, tired of being alone, tired of thinking about him, I rushed from my bed, onto the street, wearing only a cotton long-sleeved shirt that had belonged to him. I plunged into a moving van. I was knocked to the side of the road but not seriously injured.

The driver was not very sensitive and stoned me with obscenities. "Fuckin' bitch, you wanna turn me into a murderer? Fuckin' sleaze, why don't you go blow your brains out?"

In between, I'd nip around corners, sure I'd seen the back of his coat, ready to beg him to have pity on me. I wrote him a letter. "I can't live without you. I want to live with you and your new lover; I'm willing to take care of the children, wash, cook. I won't ask anything, if only I can be close to you."

I was desperate. What can I say?

He didn't answer me.

My final try. Months later, around midnight. I decided to slash my wrists. I talked on the telephone with Helena for a long time but didn't tell her anything. I was drinking heavily that night, unusual for me, and I just needed to hear a familiar voice. She suspected nothing. When we hung up, I turned on my small tape deck and put on Marvin Gaye. I put the volume way up and played the song over and over. "I want you to want me, want me too, just like I want you." I lit nine white candles and turned off the light.

By candlelight I stripped my bed and put on white sheets to match the candles. I mixed myself another gin and tonic with lime, for it was a hot mid-August night. I mixed several more; gin was a drink I was not accustomed to and I didn't know its potency.

When the wax had run over the candlesticks and onto the table, I took out a new razor blade from its container and cut deep into my left wrist. For a while I felt nothing, so I cut deeper.

I saw it before I felt it. Blood on the sheets, over the mattress, down the floor. I screamed. I stared at the blood and then at my wrist. It hurt like hell. I was going to faint. I staggered to the phone and called for help. I didn't mind dying, but, shit, I wasn't expecting it to hurt like that. So there I was on the ward again, getting patched up, waiting to get discharged. When I got home I threw out the pills I'd had to quiet my nerves. I was scared but had seen enough blood to make me never miss menstruating again.

Slowly I pulled my life and myself together. After all, it wasn't the end of the world. Just the end of a chapter with an endangered species whose manhood was at risk.

Today I still love weddings. Here I am, revelling in my cousin's future. There would be little Helenas and I'd get my chance to play part-time mother.

Compared to my wedding, Helena's was small. A handful of friends and family. Like I said, I was only the bridesmaid. The other attendant was the best man.

I wore a lovely floor-length two-piece red outfit. The skirt was long and tight-fitting, with a slit in the back leading up to the beginning of my thighs. The sleeveless top sucked over my small but upright breasts; from the waist down the top fell generously over my high firm bottom. My hair was braided in tiny plaits and held off my face by a lovely red band. The best man, Monty's cousin, wore a yellow three-piece suit a size too small for his large frame. His red tie matched my outfit and a white carnation poked out of the buttonhole on the left side of his jacket.

But I have to tell you, my cousin looked just lovely. Better than I'd ever seen her look before. Better than when she was in love with Everet Johnson. Her gown was soft and sleeveless: one-hundred per cent off-white silk. On her head was a small caplet from which flowed a white veil. That smile that could so easily turn into outrageous laughter showed perfectly white teeth. Standing there, she looked every bit the picture of virtue. Before the service began I hugged her and wished her good luck. She told me she loved me. Something in the touch of her hands made me look at her and lose myself in the beauty of her smile.

Monty wore a black three-piece suit, perfectly fitted, with a white shirt, a dark-green tie and a white carnation. His locks were caught loosely in an elastic band at the back of his neck.

Monty had wanted to marry in the Ethiopian orthodox church, but Helena insisted she had to give her parents their one wish. So the Anglican church it was. The sermon was longer than usual, for they had written their own vows. Monty was nervous, shifting from foot to foot as if his shoes were too tight. He even missed a few of his lines. Helena's voice was like the sound of a singing bird, sweet and clear. I would be a liar if I said I didn't cry tears of joy.

Then it was over and we drove to High Park to take the wedding pictures. Monty was himself again: easygoing, laid back. The camera snapped all evening: shots with Helena's parents, then with Monty's mother and sister, then me with the best man. It was glorious in the park but still very hot, and fortunate for Helena and me that our dresses were light.

By late evening it was cooler. The parents of the bride and groom left to get ready for the reception. The rest of us stayed back in the park, strolling around the flower beds, tossing confetti into the pond. I guess that was not ecologically sound, but it seemed like the thing to do.

It was almost dark when we drove off to my cousin's apartment for the reception. She had a tiny one-bedroom in a working-class Italian neighbourhood. It was above a Caribbean record shop on a busy street with cars and buses constantly on the move. The table was beautifully spread, with a white tablecloth beneath the three-layered wedding cake decorated with white icing. The rest of the cake was covered with tiny yellow, red and green flowers. The ceiling and walls of the apartment were filled with red and yellow balloons. Oh it was heavenly, but the smell of the curried goat just about overpowered the small apartment.

The speeches were long, with some embarrassing moments for my cousin and her new husband. It was, however, a festive occasion. After a few glasses of rum punch, my uncle swallowed hard and made the final speech about his baby girl, whose diapers he'd once changed. He was almost in tears by the time he got to the part where she first called him Papa and took her first steps into his arms. Through it all, my beautiful cousin sat calmly and patiently, never showing a hint of discomfort. That wonderful smile on her face. It was hard to believe that this was the same girl who pissed in the shopping mall, drove madly without a licence to Niagara Falls, stripped and danced for pleasure from Calgary to Montreal to Las Vegas.

Finally it was time for the bride and groom to dance the first song of the night. I then danced with the groom and my cousin with the best man. The parents left shortly after. Soon

I still had my red dress on as I slipped under the covers.

The last guest left and I stayed behind to help clean up. We smoked a couple of joints and picked crumbs of icing from the remainder of the wedding cake. I didn't much feel like moving from the couch, but it was their wedding night, so I reached towards the phone to call a taxi.

"What you doing?" asked Monty, casually. "Just stay over tonight. Why spend good money on a cab?" I was caught off guard and looked over to my cousin. Helena herself looked a little taken aback, but she was her old self in no time. That smile was on her face. And even I could not decipher what it meant.

"Yeah, relax. It's not like Monty and I never spent a night alone. Goodness, we've been sleeping together for the last four months." I stood up, looking at them both, still dialling for the taxi. Helena reached over and took the phone from me, hanging up. I felt some embarrassment and moved towards the door.

"No, really, stay." She held on to my arm. "Stay."

Helena helped me pull open the sofa bed, then went into the bedroom to bring sheets. Monty was leaning over me, "Why don't you join us in bed?"

I looked at him, giving him a forced smile, which actually meant are you a crazy fucker or what? Then I heard my cousin's voice, "Don't be a stranger. The bed's big enough, come on."

I couldn't read her tone— To this day I can't describe it. But I wasn't a young girl with high hopes or morals, so I went to the bedroom, and they made space for me in the middle of the bed. I still had my red dress on as I slipped under the covers. My cousin wore only her bra and panties. Monty was naked except for his underpants. I felt over-dressed and uncomfortable, yet I was secretly excited. This was out of the ordinary. Perverse in some way. We talked a bit about the wedding, the embarrassing speeches, the delicious food, the fantastic party … and then, there wasn't anything left to talk about.

I was grateful when Helena offered me a T-shirt, I relaxed a bit. Monty handed me a joint and a glass of the rum punch. We talked about who had drunk too much and who didn't drink enough and then I fell asleep to the sounds of the cars and buses below. I woke up to a warm firm hand caressing my breast, I thought I was in a dream. I enjoyed it. It was Helena's hand travelling as she slept. Then the hands became bolder and my legs were parted and met with a beard and moustache. This wasn't cousin Helena. My cousin's new husband was pulling my panties to the side. I turned towards my cousin. I tightened my legs and bottom, protesting silently. His body closed in on my behind. I pressed closer to my cousin. She must protesting silently. His body closed in on my behind. I pressed closer to my cousin. She must have heard the rustle, for her eyes opened and she turned around to catch hold of her husband's hand still tugging at my panties.

"What's the matter with this husband of yours?" I tried to sound light. "I'm going," I said, jumping towards my clothes bundled up on a chair nearby.

"Forget it, stay. It's too late to be going out. He's just a lousy fuckin' dog. Just my luck." She reached over to the night table for her pack of cigarettes. "Here, have one."

Monty was bold. He reached over to her and pulled her mouth to his. She didn't resist. He whispered something to her. I didn't hear. I was pulling hard on my cigarette. He was pulling the strap of her bra.

I was not sure what was going on, was this a ménage à trois? "Let's have another drink and a real smoke," said Monty in an unusually talkative voice.

"I'm going. I think I've had enough for one day," I said in a very high voice. I looked over to my cousin for some help.

"Stay," she said. "Let's have a drink, a joint. I'll even roll it."

I was confused. Was she accommodating Monty, or was she being entertained? Did he know about her past adventures?

Monty came back with three glasses of rum. I had a sip but could drink no more. I was beginning to see shadows of things that weren't in the room, gaudy carnival booths, riding a Ferris wheel that wouldn't stop.

Monty got out of bed and put on a Nina Simone album, one he knew was a favourite of ours. We smoked the joint slowly and he drank his rum quickly, going back for a second.

Now he was in the middle. He addressed my cousin, with a boyish grin. "You didn't give me a wedding present, you know."

She looked at him in a strange sort of way. Then that quick smile covered her pretty face. I kept smoking, perhaps a little faster, wanting to feel relaxed and very high.

She sat staring at him. The night was hot and she had thrown the covers off, showing her breasts. She lit another cigarette.

"How about giving me your cousin as a wedding present?" It was as if I weren't in the room. What had she told him?

The room was still for a while, except for Simone, going on about a thin gold ring, or something like that. It was dark too, except for the streetlights outside, but I could still see when my cousin reached over and kissed him passionately. Unpredictable that cousin of mine. But I loved her as much as I loved weddings.

His hand had no problem in finding my breast. I didn't pull away. But when his hands again tried to part my legs, I tugged at my cousin to say or do something. Helena just shrugged. She leaned over to me, her breast at my cheek. In a calm controlled voice she asked, "Do you mind fucking with him? My wedding present?"

"It's up to you, Helena," I said. "I didn't give you a present, did I?" I joked, "So if this is what you want, then it's fine by me," I said, trying to sound bold.

"Yeah. If this is the present he wants, let's make him happy."

She laughed that nervy laugh. "Let's make it memorable." I searched her eyes for some answer to this bizarre turn of events, but found none.

He wasted no time.

Monty groped for my crotch, hoisting himself on top of me. He tried to manoeuvre his cock into me. My cousin played with the tiny braids in my hair. I was beginning to enjoy this when a warm liquid poured over my face and breasts. A foul, sour smell. I cursed. My cousin jumped up and turned on the light.

"Fuckin' jerk! Bastard! You want woman and you can't even give a good fuck. Didn't just want me. Want my cousin. Asshole!" Her voice was loud, angry and full. I wondered again why she went along with it and why she married him in the first place.

Monty sat on the side of the bed in his own vomit. I felt almost sorry for him. But it was Helena's wedding night too, and she didn't ask for this. I slipped out of bed for the quiet and security of the bathroom.

I showered quickly. My cousin was dressed when I opened the bathroom door. Dressed in her wedding dress, complete with veil. I found this weird but what the hell, so was the rest of the night. I quickly dressed in my crumpled red bridesmaid's dress.

"Come on, let's go," she commanded. "I can't stand it in here."

Monty didn't say a word. He sat there looking the fool. Or cool. Or deep thinker. I don't know.

We left the apartment, walked down the street. "Let's have a drink," she said. It was way past bar hours, but we knew of several after-hours joints nearby, so arm in arm we walked towards Monroe's.

Cars slowed down to watch us, Helena in her bridal gown and veil, and me, rumpled but dressed to kill in red.

When we walked into Monroe's, the customers stared at us. The bartender came over to see if we were all right. Just fine, we assured him. No problem. We switched from the sweet syrup of the rum punch to double Scotches.

"Let's drink a toast," laughed Helena. "A toast to that fuckin' bastard, my lawful wedded husband. What did the minister say? Till death do us part? Fuck him. Fuck the minister too."

Our glasses clicked.

"Two more glasses of Scotch," my cousin Helena shouted to the bartender. Marvin Gaye was singing the song I played when I slashed my wrist.

"Let's dance, cous." We danced, Marvin in our ears: the men looked on at us. We danced long and slow.

Trish Thomas

Fuck Your Ex-Lover

Shit happens.
Life goes on.
She can find a way to get over it like we all do.
As for me,

> *I wanna turn you over and draw you up to your knees.*
> *I wanna put my middle finger and my forefinger together,*
> *slide them into your asshole,*
> *and fall deeper in love with you every time I do it.*

I don't want to apologize for that.

She can't have you,
because I have you,
simple.
Now do you want me or don't you because

> *we've got walls to press up against,*
> *restraints to buckle, harnesses to strap,*
> *and skin to cut—I wanna know you like that.*

> *I wanna see you in a black latex mini dress,*
> *long black gloves,*
> *a leather garter belt,*
> *your calves in combat boots and black seamed stockings,*
> *sitting with your thighs spread,*
> *hat on your head,*
> *elbows on your knees,*

smoking a cigarette, waiting for me to take you.

I wanna shave you bald,
yank your head back,
tie your arms above you,
clamp your nipples,
spread your legs,
hold a dildo in my hands,
and fuck you from the bottom up.

You inspire me to desire and vision
> *Can I cut a line down your back?*
> *Can I run my finger along it later,*
> *when you lay on top of me,*
> *and call it mine?*

Don't get me wrong.
I have intellectualized up the
feminist ass
with the best of them.
But all that theoretical masturbation
never got me a warm body in my bed.
It never brought me bushy legs or
musty armpits.
It never gave me sultry eyes to meet,
a wide mouth to breathe into,
or a sweet asshole to lick.
It's not gonna help me keep what I have,
or make it any more real.

I know a woman who's after my woman
when I see one
so do you want me or don't you,
because when I dare to take my hands
away from my chest
to give my heart some air,
I don't want it to be a risk,
I want it to be a gift.

> *It's you I choose to lay on my back for,*
now do you want me or don't you.

I'm Sick of It

I'm sick of taking a woman home
and finding out she can't open her legs
because her father
or her brother
or her cousin
or her uncle
or her stepfather
or her grandfather
or her mother
or her teacher or a friend of the family
or some pigs on the street
or some pigs down at the police station
already opened them for her.

I'm sick of it.

I'm sick of being understanding
and unselfish.
Sick of saying "it's ok baby"
when it's not ok.
I'm sick of not getting my way.

I'm sick of making love halfway
not touching this
avoiding that
checking in
instead of going off
somewhere new
and unknown.

I'm sick of it.

I'm sick of stopping in the middle
of everything
to cry
and recover
and change the subject
and wait til next time,

wondering if there will ever be a next time.
I'm sick of it.

I wanna do what a woman likes
not what she can barely manage
once in a while
on a good day
at the right moment
if the light's on
or the sun's not shining.

I'm sick of fighting old demons
in new lovers.

I'm sick of being rejected
and telling myself it's not really me she's saying no to.
I'm sick of telling myself I'm not gross and disgusting
unattractive and over the hill
undesirable
inept
and a bum fuck.

I'm sick of reminding myself that it's something that I have no control over
and can't change,
and I'm sick of having no control over it.

I want what I want when I want it the way I want it and
    with the woman I want it with.
    Jesus H. Christ I just wanna fucking do it.
    Is that too much to ask?

    I'm sick of taking a woman home
    and being where her father's already been.

Performers

Meryn Cadell

CHRIS BUCK

AFTER A CHEQUERED PAST THAT included French horn, ballet slippers, Super 8 films and religious musicals, Meryn Cadell emerged as a performing writer at the Beverley Tavern in Toronto in 1985. Many nightclub gigs followed, eventually leading to the release of an album, *angel food for thought,* in 1991. That in turn led to an international record deal and a modest hit on Top 40 radio in the U.S. and Canada, much to the writer's "surprise and confusion". Her second album, *bombazine,* was released on Sire/Warner in the fall of 1993. Pro-sex and anti-censorship, Cadell is currently celibate, "just for the hell of it".

Smalltime Smalltown Pamela Des Barres

The night I met the marching band
at the neighbourhood summer fair.

Trombone, saxophone, xylophone.

I go down and shake my ass.
Instrument cases litter the grass.
And after the show
you pulled your pompom pants down.

Popcorn bags and peanut shells and girls
doing highwire; I go haywire
and can't watch, so I hang with you guys
while you pack your gear.

And you pulled your pompom pants down
with the darkness all around
except those corrugated plastic lamps
stringing colour through the park
and people laugh and dribble home,
their singing receding with them
and the stars flicked out and pulled the sky up
        over us.

I stayed there and shook my ass.
Instrument cases in the grass
and you pulled your pompom pants down.
You pulled your pompom pants down.

Working Late

if you will just move your arm that way again,
against mine, in the sunshine
streaming in through the sealed windows
and our breaths on each other
and the grins gliding in next to
phenomenal fatigue

if you will just remove all your circumstance
I will do the same
to stand naked, just to talk about it
to use your fingers to indicate
and grin and sing again

And your eyes close in the marathon,
with my eyes all over you
but I avert when you're alert again,
and focus on the task at hand.

It is not proper for lust to enter
into the workplace
But the only time I fall in love
is in this forbidden space.

Where do we leave when we go from the
sealed safe sanctity of talking without doing?
We go to only lives, lonely lives
regular things like children and the dishes—

how I long to see you at my sink
or me at yours
clad in your drawers
stuck with the heat
of a summer day primed up for us
to glide up to the rooftop and fuck under the sun.

nick it in the bud

pull it open
and expose those sweet petals

then nick it, just flick it,
tiny marks to call it your own—
like pegging a wild bird
so you can find it later.

run your tongue on the scum stem,
and weird prickle of cold hot heat,

to glide
up to the
rooftop
and
fuck
under
the sun

like inside a snowsuit or so
with the wind just howling thru your hands—
and it breaks for you, waits for you,
lips parted like to speak,
but it just stares dumb
and stamen stand up oozing
and rest of it stand still.

body all bending under its weight,
petals all open and swoll'
you nick it baby
go ahead,
flick it to save it—
and later you can swallow it whole.

boy with no eyes

How do you say you're sorry
to the boy with no eyes?
How do you know how to reach him?
What if he can't realize
that when you're pushing on him
when you're pushing on his skin
that you're trying to say something to him?

He's got no ears and no connection,
just a closed smooth head.
How do you tell the boy?

How do you hold him
up to the light
to see if his ribs are broken from the storm?

I know I won't leave
until he knows that this is me.

How do you say
you're sorry
to the boy with no eyes,
except to hold his head
and just say it anyway,

then kiss his hand
even though it falls away.
The buzzing of your thinking
louder than his breathing
through the mesh
in the back
of his neck.

skin

Oh sweet skinhead,
lay your sixteen-year-old body next to mine.

You are asking me for money
on Yonge Street
and I am undressing you
with my respectable spectacles.

Sweet skinhead, you have clear eyes
and are carrying a paperback
about life in the Kingston penitentiary.

When I spread my arms wide and say,
"Look at me. Do I look like I have money?"
You say yes.
You say that you always answer yes
because everybody always says
"Look at me. Do I look like I have money?"

That makes me laugh, and you laugh too—
urchin as errant Norman Rockwell painting—
your mouth empty where your two front teeth
should be.

Sweet skinhead
I said goodbye without giving you money
but ten feet away I said:

"Okay. Fifty dollars.
What will you do for fifty dollars?"

Chicken Milk

C HICKEN MILK IS A TORONTO-BASED BAND WHOSE confectionery lyrics belie their "fast and frightening" incendiary stage presence. The band consists of Sara Montgomery and Lisa Myers on guitars and vocals, Sally Lee on bass guitar and vocals, and Laura Lee Petty on drums. They have been playing as a four-piece band since the fall of 1992, and released their debut 7" single in July of 1993 on their own Whiskey Sour Records label. Their rehearsal space is fully equipped with purple dingle balls, an autographed photo of Donny Osmond and an espresso machine. On the road, the name of the game is euchre— rhythm section vs guitars. The following lyrics were written by Sara Montgomery.

Little Dreambucket

Let you in my dreams if I
can be in yours
Passing thru in some
more fortunate time
Up on the Sun Up on the Sun
drifts off the printed page
as I stay behind

I just wanted to think nice
I just wanted to think nice
things about you

And then he came down
from the sky
Holding visions of biscuits
& chocolate pies
& I don't wanna go down there
no I don't want to go
down there

All that's left is imagination
& mood-ring eyes
ripplin' through my loneliest times
Satan Be Gone Satan Be Gone
smears the printed page
as I send the prayer

I just wanted to think nice
I just wanted to think nice
things about you

& then she threw
her dreams to the sun
sayin' I can do better
than these ones
I ask my little dreambucket
I ask my little dreambucket

who is true anyway

Amusing

No time for things that
came and went
and hours of justification
conquer my muse
and her hedonist ways
to leave her in the gutter
and here you want my gratitude
for all that you have
taught me
clear away the attitude
that someone else has
bought me

come in your ethereal vanity
that of wanton lover
that of rocket fuelled nights
a cheap con coveting credit
for involuntary fires

No time again your ploy revealed
no Beatrice-like infatuation
selling my soul for less viable goals
still thinking you're really clever
no longer in my servitude
the reason for your existence
the ploy's revealed as
really crude
and weak to my resistance

Come in your temporal vanity
that of wanton lover
that of rocket fuelled nights
the cheap con coveting credit
for involuntary fires
but me I'm not waiting
for it.

Outside My Window

Standing in my room listening to the trees
sway outside my window.
You say Okay give me a hug and I'll
be on my way.
The only thing I can remember is the
Pain from holding on so tight.
Pain from holding on too tight.
Standing in my room listening to the trees
sway outside my window.
Our friendship has grown to a silence in my
heart now. Our friendship has grown to a silence.
The call I wanted to make that day
made my feelings change, made my feelings change.
Funny what fear can do to me
it made my feelings change.
And the only thing I can remember is the
Pain from holding on so tight.
Pain from holding on too tight.
I'm inside my room listening to the trees
sway outside my window.
Called your number there was never
an answer.
Really you have nothing to say to my lies.
I've got something to tell you
my lies were the way I
delivered the message.
And YAH I'm holding on so tight.
     YAH I'm holding on too tight.

Cookie Cream

And then he took me out
& we went down to the picture show
& I thought what can I eat
while watching Robert De Niro
It's the sweetness I can taste & roll on my tongue

Give me the cookie cream now
Give me the cookie cream
I want it in me
I want it in me

I close my eyes & it all seems clear to me
what my streets were paved with
what strange fruit on the trees
where dentists die slow & painful fates
& cookies don't come stuffed with stupid things
     like dates

Give me the cookie cream now
Give me the cookie cream
I want it in me
I want it in me

If I had it my way I'd eat what's in between
That's the way it turned out in my other cookie
     dreams
But now these cookie dreams are turning into a
     nightmare
But now these cookie dreams are turning into a
     nightmare

Then he gathered me up with his lips
& we went somewhere soft & warm
where biscuits don't stand in the way of sweetness
     galore
I found my hand caught in the mouth of your
     cookie jar
I found my heart lodged in the bottom of your
     honey jar

Give me the cookie cream now
Give me the cookie cream now
I want it in me
I want it in me

Fifth Column

JENA VON BRUCKEN

THE MOTHERS OF ALL RIOT GRRRLS, FIFTH COLUMN released their first "bubblegum rebellion" album, *To Sir With Hate,* in 1985. Since then, they have contributed to the soundtracks of alternative films and have themselves been the subject of two films: John Porter's performance film *Fifth Column* and Bruce la Bruce's docu-drama *All Time Queen of the World,* which was released in conjunction with Fifth Column's second album ("All Time Queen of the World") in 1990. Most recently, they joined the 1993 Lollapalooza tour for several of its Canadian dates.

It's a Really Weird Thing

[AZAR / BRECKENRIDGE]

EXTERIOR. *An empty town street after the rain. Night.*
A blob of energy makes its way into the frame. STEVE *is leav-*
ing his apartment.

FEMALE VOICE
    Look out!
STEVE
    What the hell is that?

A female chorus of goblins appears.

GOBLINS
    And it's just too much
    And afraid to touch
    And goes downtown
    And does not make a sound
    And turning around
    And looking at you
    And wondering what to do
    And coming right this way
    I don't know what to say
    And it's busting out
    And it's gotta shout
    And there's just no doubt
    That you best look out

[*Take a deep breath now.*]

    It's not telling anyone
    All the creepy things it's done
    It's turning black and blue
    And its heart is beating too
    It won't go away
    And it wants to play
    And it's sticky
    And it's got a hickey
    And it whirls and twirls
    And it jumps and swirls

    And it makes me spin
    And it does me in
    And it's dripping wet
    And I'll just bet
    It won't go away
    And it wants to play
    You can't run away
    Cause today's the day
    This thing came to stay
    This thing came to stay
    It's a really weird thing
    The thing that made love
    It's a really weird thing
    Whoa!
    It's a really weird thing
    The thing that made love
    It's a really weird thing
    Whoa!

Suddenly the blob transforms into a beautiful, tall, large,
adolescent, red-headed girl. STEVE *is devastated, shaking for*
dear life.

RED-HEAD
    You better learn how to swim and you better learn fast
    Cause there are some big waves that are ready to crash
    I'm a real whirlpool and you're gonna go under
    Look out for the rain and the thunder

STEVE *is choking and drowning in his own sweat.*

RED-HEAD
    You can't hide
    You can't run from the flood
    You're gonna slip and slide
    In ten feet of mud
    It's a really weird thing
    The thing that made love
    Whoa!

All Women Are Bitches
[AZAR / JONES]

Which are more dangerous,
men or guns?
Both are dangerous
But only a man can kill you,
or at least try

All women are …
All women are …
All women are …
All women are …

So your husband took your babies
He doesn't want to set you free

Hey the best thing you
could do would be to
move in with me

We could split the rent
We could split the fun

Take a look at the situation
Tell yourself that all women are …

Don't be so angry honey
Don't you be so sad
Don't be so angry honey
Things can't be all that bad

Wanna make a bet?
I don't like the way yo' boyfriend
looks at me
Oh ya!
I don't like the smell of his aftershave
and he reeks of suspicion as well
Well oh yeah—Can you blame him?
(All women are …)

Oh ya!

Can you blame him?

I know what he's thinking
All women are …

Don't be so angry honey
Don't you be so sad
Don't be so angry honey
Things can't be all that bad

And look here he comes now with his
five-hundred-dollar kind of suit
He's so cute?
He's got a lotta loot

And there he goes draggin' junior
out to the cherry orchard,
tellin' him the facts of life,
"look son, just cause mom gets angry sometimes …

"don't take it personally son, because …"
"cause why dad?"
"cause all women are bitches, son"
"really dad?"
All women are …

Don't be so angry honey
Don't you be so sad
Don't be so angry honey
Things can't be all that bad
All women are bitches …

Get the Bug

[AZAR]

There was a doctor whose name does int madder
He was a shrink he was a grump
Then one day there was someone on his couch
Who called him a grouch
Crazy mad patient made a funny face
The doctor then asked does this relate?

He got the bug ya!
He got the bug ya!
He got the bug ya!
He got the bug ya!

Postgirl on the run's got a kink in her brain
Always bitches about the rain
Asked her how she felt about the sleet and snow
You ask me that question again and again
Stormy weather teaches us humility
I guess that's why I hate my job
And that's what she said was wrong with the rain
Nevertheless in the midst of a shower she felt the power

She got the bug ya!
She got the bug ya!
She got the bug ya!
She got the bug ya!

Got to get money at the bank
The teller's got a roll of pennies up his ass
Makes a stink about a welfare cheque
Says we're not playing with a full deck
He hates his three-piece suit
He wants your latex suit
He wants some freedom

Mug bug ... what's the bug ... not the love bug ...

Got the bug ya he got the bug ya!
Got the bug ya he got the bug ya!

Got the bug ya he got the bug ya!
Got the bug ya he got the bug ya!

And now he's the Queen of the Scene
      nightmare
But now these cookie dreams are turning into a
      nightmare

Then he gathered me up with his lips
& we went somewhere soft & warm
where biscuits don't stand in the way of sweetness
      galore
I found my hand caught in the mouth of your
      cookie jar
I found my heart lodged in the bottom of your
      honey jar

Give me the cookie cream now
Give me the cookie cream now
I want it in me
I want it in me

Sahara Spracklinn

PATTI SUDAN

SAHARA SPRACKLINN IS A POET/PERFORMER AND
self-styled anar(t)ist, with a dangerous edge she attrib-
utes to having Uranus in the Tenth House. She has been
performing (with her electric guitar or Las Vegas-style sequinned
acoustic) in Ontario and Quebec for sixteen years, at many
venues including the University of Toronto's Convocation
Hall's "Manifestival", The Stratford Festival and Harbourfront.
She has also performed and organized music and poetry cabarets
at many Toronto clubs. Spracklinn's performances are leg-
endary: her axe-wielding presence on local stages always ensures
an evening of theatre, drama, insight and festiveness. For a recent
Christmas performance, she arrayed herself and her mohawk
in tinsel and ornaments, while delivering a devastating mono-
logue about the women on "Star Trek" who never appear to
suffer from PMS.

Eroticar

The car's barely warmed up.
He's putting his hands on the gears.
Very smooth. But I eased off. Fear of
high octane fuel. A wonderful feeling
my heart was pounding glass or metal.
Zone-moaned, new, glass-heated arguments
moaned too hard, most exotic like a beautiful
woman. A beautiful woman last seen walking
from behind. Pull over to the side and turn
off the ignition. So I park it on the street
and turn off the ignition. His red rocket
warmed up gobbling high octane, gun-designed
guitar body, skeletal frame insured for thousands of
dollars and it's only metal, warmed up, like a
beautiful woman: exotic . hard . metal .

xx

ooooo

You'll understand why I had to let him go: his red
rocket stuck too hard. I moaned exotic, still trying
to act my way out of the pain. Because my heart
was pounding. Pounding me into the ground. But he
eased off. Zone-struck. That speed! Capable of hit-
ting hard! Glass or metal! O God!
My heart was pounding
was pounding a wonderful feeling. Politically it didn't
matter, who was driving and who was steering.

O.D.'d On Your Mouth

I will imagine that your mouth
now tastes of spring/onions, Robert
not by chance, by choice, in that you have just
eaten one.
I will imagine that you are
still in your one-room apartment
cock in hand, pissing into your dirty
toilet bowl that I cleaned once,
Florence Nightingale that I was.
The concrete of the street being too hard
for your feet, I will picture you
on the recline. The city is right in
the centre of you now
and all the traffic has stopped
just in time to save your life.
But you still dart in and out
on your bicycle between the cars.
I imagine you feel a little like showing
off your cock size
to any female passerby: cocksure
in that outgoing way of yours: up
to your ears in girls
jutting: up some alleyway
and you ride the wild energy
running between a woman's thighs
like a bolt of strong skylight
or a spool of dazzling thread,
your generosity unwinds, and it leaves
only nothing, but a poem behind

Wounded at Love

Wounded at love, shot
down to my rightful place a woman
in a man's life, asleep
he forgets her face

mad
you're driving me to madness or murder
for better or for worser
a triple-pack homicide/momicide/patricide

you can take your parents with you
eggface—you can be the perfect son
whose fingers are wet
from bullets and caged dreams

only when you're on top of me
do you give me something
that already doesn't belong to me

go and hump a tree
those little stumps that were once limbs
(my thalidomide arms) wounded at love
reaching out for you again and again
will. take. you. in

Janet Stone

RON BOUDREAU

JANET STONE STARTED SINGING AND WRITING LYRICS
more than ten years ago during a high-school video project
and has since been in numerous bands. During the heyday of
Queen Street in Toronto in the early 1980s, her band Echo
Papa (named after Elvis Presley's airplane signal) was often fea-
tured at the Beverley Tavern on its Elvis Mondays, cabaret nights
featuring proto-thrash bands and any number of spontaneous jams
or groups. Stone formed Whipping Post in 1988 after completing
her undergraduate degree in English and Creative Writing at
York University, where she co-founded the alternative magazine
Off the Pigs. Stone is now forming an all-girl thrash band called
The Axe Murderers, in which she hopes to perform the Michael
Des Barres glitter-song "I'll Bang You, Baby, With My Heavy,
Heavy Hammer."

Whip me

i love the way you used to whip me
whip me with a single glance
i love the way you used to whip me
whip me around when we danced

i would have done anything to stay with your grasp
i would have bent over backwards
i would have done anything you asked

chorus

you vowed your love it came in a letter
a spectre in my dreams
reality is better
you promised me bliss
i should have insisted
you promised me pleasure
i should have resisted
you

i love the way you used to whip me
whip me with a single glance
i love the way you used to whip me
whip me around when we danced

i feel like i have been branded
branded by your hands
you left me stranded
you are a cruel man

chorus

you vowed your love it came in a letter
a spectre in my dreams
reality is better
you promised me bliss
i should have insisted
you promised me pleasure
i should have resisted
you

refrain

in this playground we call desire
you made me a promise
but you are a liar
yes you are a liar

i would have done anything to stay within your grasp
i would have bent over backwards
i would have done anything you asked

chorus

you vowed your love it came in a letter
a spectre in my dreams
reality is better
you promised me bliss
i should have insisted
you promised me pleasure
i should have resisted
you

Burn

burn, burn baby i burn
burn, burn baby i burn
you touch my hand you're desire
burn me
i am an ember

cry, cry baby i cry
cry, cry, cry with delight
you open your lips you're desire
hear me
i am a flicker

chorus

energy abounds in your eyes evergreen
you look at me and i fall down
embrace surround everyone envies
you touch me and i fall down
obsess me, possess me

obsess me, possess me
and i will fall down

burn, burn baby i burn
burn, burn baby i burn
caress my skin you're desire
burn me
i have ignited

scream, scream baby i scream
scream, scream baby i scream
i open my legs
lift me higher
burn me
i have extinguished

chorus
    spirit elevates see the ebb and flow
    you look at me and i fall down
    everyday is new experience
    you touch me and i fall down
    obsess me, possess me
    obsess me, possess me
    and i will fall down

Deep Within

i want to caress every pore of your skin and cover
    your body with mine
i want to unlock all your hidden treasures and bury
    my face in your gems

i want to describe your rainbow eyes so the rest of
    the world can see
the gunmetal grey, the hyacinth blue, the
    mysterious shade of green

chorus
    i want you deep within my skin
    i want you deep within my skin

    i want you deep
    within my skin

i want to tell you every secret i've kept and i want
    you to feel the same
i want to carry you to a faraway place and engulf yo
    in my embrace

chorus
    i want you deep within my skin
    i want you deep within my skin
    i want you deep
    within my skin

refrain
sometimes you're distant
sometimes you're cruel
your moods swing
and i try to follow you
you make me feel like
i'm a fool and i'm no fool

chorus
    i want you deep within my skin
    i want you deep within my skin
    i want you deep
    within my skin

    my skin

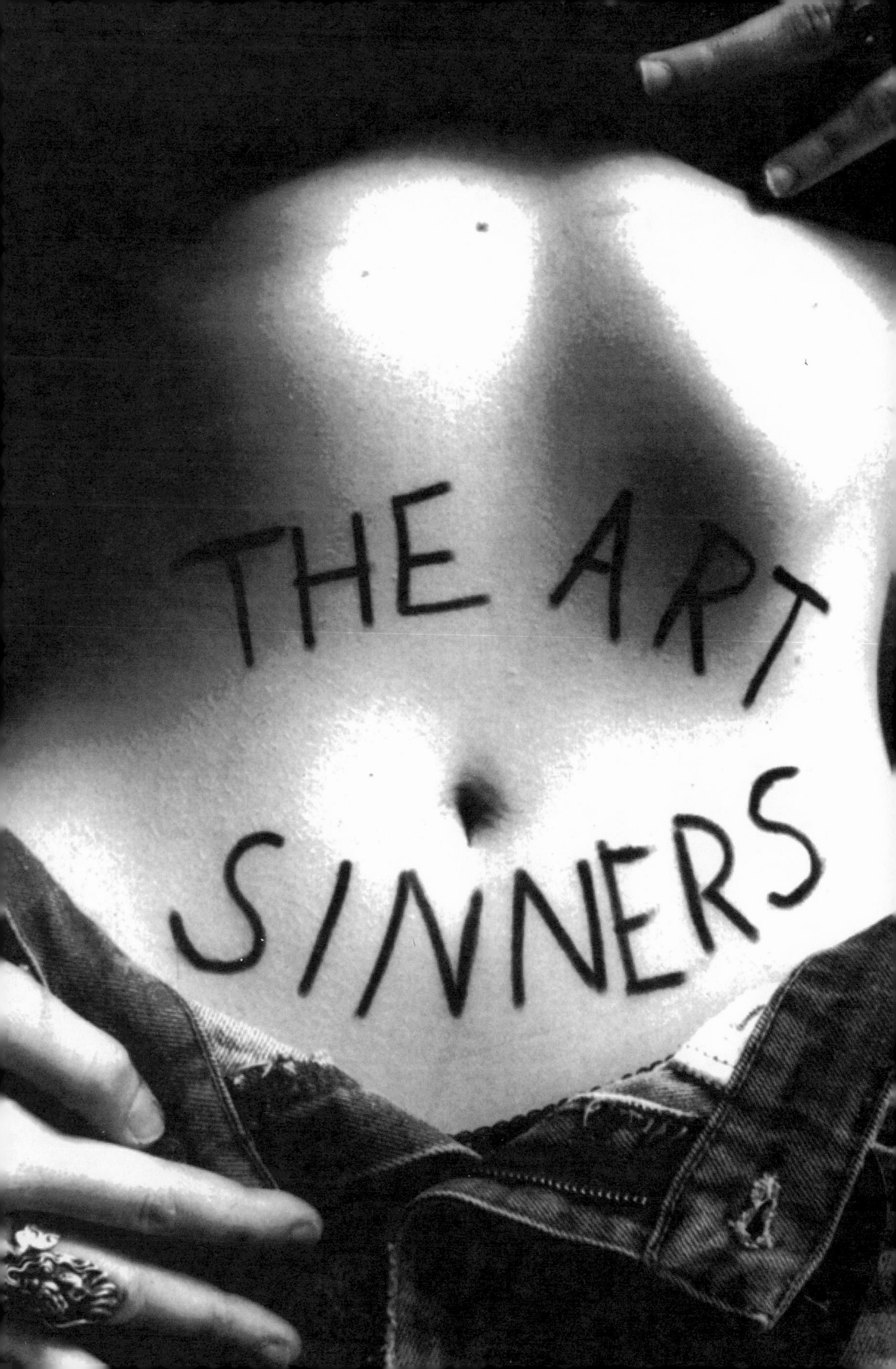
THE ART
SINNERS

KATHY ACKER's books include *Blood and Guts in High School, Great Expectations, Empire of the Senseless* and *The Childlike Life of the Black Tarantula.* Her work has also appeared in a variety of anthologies including *The New Gothic, High Risk* and *The Seven Deadly Sins.* She lives in San Francisco.

MARY LOUISE ADAMS's writing has appeared in fiction and non-fiction anthologies and in magazines and journals including *Fuse, Fireweed, NOW* and *Herizons.* Her work is contextualized by many years of participation in the lesbian, feminist and AIDS movements.

BETH BRANT is a Bay of Quinte Mohawk from Tyendinaga Mohawk Territory in Ontario. She is the editor of *A Gathering of the Spirit,* a collection of writing and art by Native woman, and the author of *Mohawk Trail,* prose and poetry, and *Food & Spirits,* short stories. Her work has appeared in numerous Native, feminist and lesbian anthologies. She is currently working on a book of essays, and a collection of her speeches, *Good, Red Roads,* is forthcoming. She contributes to her communities through writing workshops, mentoring programs and working with Native women in prison to help develop their creative voice. She is a mother and grandmother. She lives in Michigan.

NICOLE BROSSARD has published more than twenty books. A poet, novelist and essayist, she co-founded the literary magazine *La Barre du Jour* and the feminist newspaper *Les Têtes de Pioche.* She also co-directed the film *Some American Feminists* and recently co-edited *Anthologie de la poésie des femmes au Québec.* She has twice received the Governor General's Award for Poetry and has been awarded both the Harbourfront Festival Prize and the Prix Anthanase-David for her body of work. She lives in Montreal.

REBECCA BROWN is the author of *Annie Oakley's Girl, The Terrible Girls, The Haunted House* and *The Children's Crusade.* She lives in Seattle.

ROBYN CAKEBREAD is an English and Philosophy major at the University of Toronto. She is a recovering drug addict, who has lived in and around Toronto all her life. In her work she explores the rift between fiction and confession, with a special focus on the multiplicity of female sexuality. This is her first publication.

CHANTALE DOYLE lives in Montreal with a fish named Alex and a cat named Pierre. She spends her days making necklaces out of plastic fruit and vegetables, elaborately carved dragons out of popsicle sticks, tuques and mittens for Alex and Pierre and comic books. To order her comics, write to her at Box 42033, Montreal, Quebec H2W 2T3.

PAMELA DES BARRES is the author of *I'm With the Band* and *Take Another Little Piece of My Heart.* She was one of the members of Girls Together Outrageously (the GTO's), a 1960s rock band. She is now at work on a subversive account of the life of Mary Magdalene and "His Nibs". She lives in Santa Monica.

ANN DIAMOND is a Montreal poet, novelist and journalist whose works include *Lil, A Nun's Diary, Mona's Dance, Snakebite, Terrorist Letters, Evil Eye* and *Static Control. A Nuns Diary* was adapted for theatre by director Robert LePage. The resulting play, "Echo", was the subject of a recent film, *Breaking a Leg,* directed by Donald Winkler.

Mona's Dance was adapted as a dance performance by Leslie-Ann Coles of Toronto and *Lil* was adapted as "Lil: A Dance Western" by Montreal dancer and choreographer Janet Oxley.

JULIE DOUCET was first published in magazines such as *Weirdo, Wimmen's Comix, Rip Off Comix* and *Drawn & Quarterly*. She has been producing her own solo comic book, *Dirty Plotte*, since 1991, and is now working on issue No 8. She lives in Montreal. To order *Dirty Plotte*, write to Drawn & Quarterly, 5550 Jeanne Mance St., Montreal, Quebec H2V 4K6.

RAMABAI ESPINET is a Trinidadian by birth and has lived in Canada for many years. Her published works include the collection of poetry *Nuclear Seasons*, the anthology *Creation Fire*, which she edited, and a children's book, *The Princess of Spadina*.

ELLEN R. FLANDERS is a Jewish lesbian photo-essayist and anti-censorship activist. Much of her photography centres on Middle East issues, anti-semitism and queer struggles. Her work has been exhibited across Canada and abroad and has been published in various journals. She is a member of the editorial collective of *Fireweed: a feminist quarterly of writing, politics, art and culture*. She lives in Toronto.

MARY GAITSKILL is the author of *Bad Behavior*, a short-fiction collection, and *Two Girls, Fat and Thin*, a novel. Her critical and literary work has appeared in anthologies and magazines including *Details, Esquire* and *High Risk*. She lives in San Francisco.

GIGI THE GALAXY GIRL, a.k.a. Nancy Johnston, finds creative inspiration for her short stories through her involvement in science-fiction fandom. She is the co-founder and editor of *Science Friction*, a Star Trek fiction zine. She lives in Toronto.

BARBARA GOWDY is a writer and editor whose books are *The Rabbit and the Hare, Through the Green Valley, Falling Angels* and *We So Seldom Look On Love*. Her short stories are included in the anthologies *Best American Short Stories 1989, Slow Hand: Women Writing Erotica* and *Best American Erotica 1993*. She lives in Toronto.

ROBERTA GREGORY has been creating alternative comics for almost twenty years. Her earliest work appeared in *Wimmen's Comix* #4 in 1974. In 1976, she became the first woman to solo write, draw, publish and distribute a comic book, *Dynamite Damsels*. She has contributed extensively to *Gay Comix* and is now best known for her comic book series *Naughty-Bits*, in which the story in this volume first appeared. For a catalogue of her current comics, send a SASE (US postage) to: Roberta Gregory, P.O. Box 27438, Seattle, WA 98125.

SANDRA HAAR writes, speaks and presents in the areas of culture, identity, race and sexuality and is a member of the *Fireweed* collective. "This is impenetrable anatomy ..." was exhibited (in its full form) at Gallery 76 in 1990. "Who is a princess ..." was exhibited in *Sex and Identity* at Artefact Gallery in 1991 and printed in *Fireweed's* special issue on Jewish women (#35, 1992). She lives in Toronto.

XAVIERA HOLLANDER is the Dutch author of *The Happy Hooker*, a book that has sold 16 million copies in various languages. Her column "Call Me Madam" appears regularly in *Penthouse* magazine, and she is a sought after lecturer and commentator. She has published more than a dozen books, including *Xaviera's Super Sex, Xaviera's Magic Mushrooms, Fiesta of the Flesh* and *The Golden Phallus of Osiris*, and has produced two albums. Hollander believes "the voice" is the primary erogenous zone and urges communication about sexual issues including AIDS awareness, eroticism and sexual pleasure and problems.

CASSIE JAMESON is a sixteen-year-old "riot grrrl" from North Carolina. Like the majority of her sisters in subversion, she likes to create public scenes and (re)face public property with radical grrrl-slogans. She has a keen interest in women's history, women's thrash bands such as Hole and Babes in Toyland, feminist praxis and (to cite Bikini Kill) "Revolution Girl Style".

MIRIAM JONES is the author of the chapbook *Couplings: Four Stories*. She has also published pieces in *Acta Victoriana, Border/Lines, Catalyst, Diva, (f.)Lip, Paragraph, Rampike, Rites* and *Rubicon*. She is currently working on a collection of short fiction about the body. She lives in Toronto.

ERICA JONG is the author of a number of novels, including *Fear of Flying* and *How to Save Your Own Life*, and volumes of poetry, most recently *Becoming Light*. She is also known as a critical writer, a public speaker and a biographer. She lives in New York.

EVELYN LAU 's first book was *Runaway*, an autobiographical account of her experiences as a street kid and aspiring poet in the mid 1980s. She has since written three books of poetry, *You Are Not Who You Claim, Oedipal Dreams* (short-listed for the Governor General's Award) and the forthcoming *In the House of Slaves*. Her new collection of short fiction is entitled *Fresh Girls*. She lives in Vancouver.

CAROL LAZARE was an award-winning actor for twelve years; after her daughter Lilly was born, she found she wanted to create characters, not just portray them, and she turned to writing. "Addicted to Love," the piece included here, is an excerpt from a screenplay-in-progress. She lives in Toronto.

LYDIA LUNCH has, since the age of sixteen, continuously assaulted complacency via music, film, spoken word and writing. Her writing includes *Adulterer's Anonymous*, a collaborative book of poetry written with Exene Cervenka, *Incriminating Evidence*, a collection of stories, rants and scripts, and *As-Fix-E-8*, a comic illustrated by Mike Mathews. Spoken-word recordings include *The Uncensored Lydia Lunch, Oral Fixation* and *Conspiracy of Women*. She lives in Los Angeles.

CAREL MOISEIWITSCH's work has appeared in a variety of publications including the *L.A. Times* and the *Village Voice*. She has had several exhibitions across Canada, and her art has been the subject of articles by critics Lucy Lippard and Robin Laurence, among others. She lives in Vancouver.

DAWN MOURNING is a Toronto-based writer who began writing and publishing erotica chapbooks in 1979. A registered self-publisher who does not give readings or submit her work to mainstream publications, she publishes her books in limited editions of 100 copies, and each book has been sold out, thanks to word of mouth and her devoted following. She has published fourteen books, including *Ball Parings, Dressed to Kill, Toilet Trained at Last, Rapture 13* and *Proud Profane and Pornographic.*

SYLVIE RANCOURT worked as a stripper in Montreal for ten years, until the birth of her first child. In 1985, she became the first Canadian woman to self-publish her own comic magazine, *Mélody,* the true story of her life as a nude dancer. Originally written in French, *Mélody* now appears in an expanded English version illustrated and translated by Jacques Boivin and published by Kitchen Sink Press. She lives in Abitibi.

SUZY RICHTER's Super 8 film *Cross Your Heart,* which is excerpted here in part, was screened in 1991 in Toronto, at the Purple Institute, and at festivals in London and Berlin. It is appearing at the 7th Annual New York Lesbian and Gay Film Festival in Fall 1993. Richter co-founded the band The Nancy Sinatras and was its lead singer from 1988 to 1993. She lives in Toronto.

PATRICIA SEAMAN has published a novel, *Hotel Destiné,* and a chapbook, *Amphibian Hearts;* a book of short stories, *Divine Words,* is forthcoming. Her work has been anthologized in *Coming Attractions 91, 90: Best Canadian Stories* and in *Imagining Women* and has appeared in many periodicals including *Paragraph, Open Letter, Border/Lines, What* and *Descant.* She lives in Toronto.

MAKEDA SILVERA spent her early years in Kingston, Jamaica, before immigrating to Canada. Her stories, articles and essays have appeared in numerous journals and magazines. She is the author of *Silenced,* a book of oral interviews with Caribbean domestic workers in Canada, and *Remembering G,* a collection of short stories; her second story collection, *Her Head a Village,* is forthcoming. She edited *Piece of My Heart,* a lesbians-of-colour anthology, and is the co-founder of Toronto's Sister Vision Press.

FIONA SMYTH's paintings pop up on restaurant and club walls as often as at galleries; since 1986 her recognizable style has grown like ivy over Toronto and has graced magazine pages as well as comics, including her comic book *Nocturnal Emissions.*

LISA SAKULENSKY's photographs have appeared in periodicals including *Our Time, Parachute* and *Justice,* and at galleries in Vancouver and Toronto. Her work on The International Ladies Garment Worker's Union has had several Toronto exhibitions including *Imagining Labour* in 1991 and *Stitches in Time: A Show of Archival and Original Photographs* in 1993.

TRISH THOMAS is a career-minded, patronizing, officious adversarial prima donna who thinks she deserves special treatment. Ask anybody. Her work has appeared in *Bad Attitude, Fireweed, Frighten the Horses, Invert, Slippery When Wet, Taste of Latex, The Sandmutopia Guardian* and *Wicked Women.* Her work has also been anthologized in *Best American Erotica 1993* and *Dagger.* She lives in San Francisco.

BARBARA WILSON is the author of a number of lesbian detective novels that include her Pam Nilsen series, *Murder in the Collective, Sisters of the Road* and *The Dog Collar Murders.* She is currently completing a mystery set in Romania, entitled *Trouble in Transylvania.* She is the co-publisher of Seal, a Seattle-based press.

*Grateful acknowledgement is made to the following
for permission to reprint from previously published material:*

Acker, Kathy. "New York City in 1979" © 1991 by Kathy Acker, All Rights Reserved. Reprinted from *Hannibal Lecter, My Father* by permission of the William Morris Agency, Inc. on behalf of the author.
Adams, Mary Louise. "Episode 1: Citric Encounter" © 1986 by Mary Louise Adams. Reprinted from *Rites*, July-August 1986, by permission of the author.
—————. "Episode 2" © 1989 by Mary Louise Adams. Reprinted from *Fireweed*, number 28, Spring 1989, by permission of the author.
Brossard, Nicole. "Reverse/Drift" and "A Rod for a Handsome Price" © 1980 by Nicole Brossard. Translated by Larry Shouldice. Reprinted from *Daydream Mechanics* by permission of the author.
—————. Excerpts from *French Kiss* © 1986 by Nicole Brossard. Translated by Patricia Claxton. Reprinted by permission of the author.
Brown, Rebecca. "Isle of Skye" © 1990 by Rebecca Brown. Reprinted from *The Terrible Girls* by permission of City Lights Books.
Diamond, Ann. "A Journal of Mona" © 1979 by Ann Diamond. Reprinted from *Canadian Forum*, January-February 1979, by permission of the author.
Doucet, Julie. "It's Clean Up Time!" © 1991 by Julie Doucet. Reprinted from *Dirty Plotte*, number 4, by permission of the artist.
Gaitskill, Mary. "The Rose Taboo" © 1992 by Mary Gaitskill. Reprinted from *Details*, July 1992, by permission of the author.
Gowdy, Barbara. "We So Seldom Look On Love" © 1993 by Barbara Gowdy. Reprinted from *We So Seldom Look On Love* by permission of the author and of HarperCollins Publishers Inc.
Gregory, Roberta. "Bitchy Bitch Gets Laid" © 1991 by Roberta Gregory. Reprinted from *Naughty Bits*, number 1, by permission of the artist.
Jong, Erica. "Fruits & Vegetables" © 1971 by Erica Mann Jong. All rights reserved. Reprinted from *Fruits & Vegetables* by permission of the poet.
—————. "Love Magick" © 1981 by Erica Mann Jong. Reprinted from *Witches* by permission of Harry N. Abrams Inc.
—————. "The Long Tunnel of Wanting You" © 1977 by Erica Mann Jong. Reprinted from *How To Save Your Own Life* by permission of Henry Holt and Company Inc.
Lau, Evelyn. "Mercy" © 1992 by Evelyn Lau. Reprinted from *Fresh Girls and Other Stories* by Evelyn Lau. Published in Canada by HarperCollins Publishers Ltd. First published in a slightly different form in *Left Bank* magazine. Published in the United States by Hyperion Books (1994). Used by permission of the author.
Moiseiwitsch, Carel. Devils Live in a Quiet Pond © 1992. Reprinted from *L.A. Weekly* by permisson of the artist.
Mourning, Dawn. Poems © 1981 by Dawn Mourning. Reprinted from *Proud Profane and Pornographic* by permission of the author.
Rancourt, Sylvie and Jacques Boivin. "From the Bottom" © 1993 by Sylvie Rancourt and Jacques Boivin. Reprinted from *Melody*, number 6, by permission of Kitchen Sink Press and the author.
Seaman, Patricia. "The Dress" © 1991 by Patricia Seaman. Reprinted from *Amphibian Hearts* by permission of the author.
Thomas, Trish. "Fuck Your Ex-Lover" © 1991 by Trish Thomas. Reprinted from *Taste of Latex*, number 7, by permission of the author.
—————. "I'm Sick of It" © 1990 by Trish Thomas. Reprinted from *Frighten the Horses*, Summer 1990, by permission of the author.
Wilson, Barbara. Excerpt from *The Dog Collar Murders* © 1989 by Barbara Wilson. Reprinted by permission of the author.